POSTMODERNITY
AND EUROPEAN EDUCATION
SYSTEMS
CULTURAL DIVERSITY AND
CENTRALIST KNOWLEDGE

David Coulby and Crispin Jones

Trentham Books

First published in 1995 by Trentham Books Limited

Trentham Books Limited
Westview House
734 London Road
Oakhill
Stoke-on-Trent
Staffordshire
England ST4 5NP

British Cataloguing in Publication Data
A catalogue record for this book is available from the British Library.

ISBN: 1 85856 033 0

Cover: Inscription No.18 (etching) by John Stipling

Designed and typeset by Trentham Print Design Limited, Chester and printed in Great Britain by Bemrose Shafron Limited, Chester

Acknowledgements

This book came about because we wanted to explain to ourselves what seemed to be happening to education in Europe after the collapse of state socialism. The scope of the book changed as we worked on it and, to help in the clarification of our ideas, most of the chapters had their early origins in papers presented at conferences and seminars across Europe. We therefore owe a great debt to friends and colleagues for the constructive comments that they made on these papers, helping us to clarify our ideas as well as bringing new lines of enquiry to our attention. This process has meant that the book has been a long time in the writing, so long that we are almost sorry to finish it. Our thanks to the many people who have given us help and advice about it over the last three years or so.

CONTENTS

Chapter One   1
MODERNISM AND EDUCATION: 'THEORISING ITS OWN
CONDITION OF POSSIBILITY'

Chapter Two   11
CLASS, 'RACE' AND EDUCATIONAL ACHIEVEMENT

2.1. Xenophobia in a Uniting Europe   11
2.2. Educational Systems and Differential Achievement   13
2.3. Curricular Systems and Differential Attainment   16

Chapter Three   23
MODERNIST KNOWLEDGE AND NATIONAL
CURRICULUM SYSTEMS

3.1. Modernist Knowledge   23
3.2. The Collapse of Modernist Knowledge   32
3.3. The State Enforcement of Modernist Knowledge   37

Chapter Four   41
THE EDUCATIONAL CONSTRUCTION OF EUROPE

4.1. 'The Reverse of Europe'   41
4.2. 'The Extent of Their Dominions'   44
4.3. 'Marked out by Nature'   50

Chapter Five   59
EUROPEAN CIVIC CULTURE: TRADITIONAL AND
MODERNIST

5.1. Civic Culture and International Urbanisation   59
5.2. Semiology and the City   64
5.3. Traditionalist European Civic Culture   67
5.4. European Civic Culture and the Curriculum   72

Chapter Six   79
DIFFERENTIATION AND MODERNITY

6.1. Human Rights and the Political Definition of Minorities   79
6.2. Education Systems and Differentiation   83
6.3. Educational Differentiation and Minority Languages   89

Chapter Seven   95
**ETHNOCENTRICITY, POSTMODERNITY AND EUROPEAN
KNOWLEDGE SYSTEMS**

7.1. European Knowledge Systems and Ethnocentricity   95
7.2. Traditional and Modern Knowledge Systems in the School and   99
University Curriculum
7.3. Postmodern Knowledge as Critique: Cultural Relativism   102
7.4. The Curricular Possibilities of Postmodernism   106

Chapter Eight   111
**NEW, OR MAKING THE SAME MISTAKES? RACISM,
REFUGEES AND INTERCULTURAL EDUCATION IN
EUROPE**

8.1. Progressive Taxonomies and Oscillating Policies   111
8.2. 'Owing to Well Founded Fear of Being Persecuted'   116
8.3. The Education of Refugees in the UK   121

Chapter Nine   127
EUROPEAN CULTURE: UNITY AND FRACTURES

9.1. 'To strengthen the Spirit of European Citizenship'   127
9.2. Regional, National and European Cultures: Beyond the   129
Folklore Museum
9.3. International Migration and European Culture: Empires   133
and Error
9.4. Nationalist Knowledge   138

Chapter Ten   141
POSTMODERNITY AND EDUCATIONAL POLICY

Bibliography   149

Index   165

Chapter One

MODERNISM AND EDUCATION: 'THEORISING ITS OWN CONDITION OF POSSIBILITY'

The distinction between modernity and postmodernity seems to have as many definitions as there are writers on the topic. Furthermore, it is a distinction which has, in the main, been developed in academic areas well away from educational studies. It is necessary, then, to emphasise what this book is and is not about. It is not an attempt to extrapolate from architectural, literary, sociological and cultural studies' theorising about the nature of modernity, a definition of postmodernity, and then to apply this to European education systems. This in itself would be a modernist, if fascinating, endeavour. Nor is it an attempt to form systematic generalisations about the way in which the concept of postmodernism may be applied to education, (although interestingly, in the long preparation of this book, at least two other titles linking education and postmodernity have emerged (Aronowitz and Giroux, 1991; Usher and Edwards, 1994); the second of these does, to an extent, attempt this task). The concept of postmodernity itself is, however, too diverse, fractured and self-conscious, to allow for such a systematic approach. As Jameson notes,

> Postmodernism, Postmodern consciousness, may then amount to no more than theorising its own condition of possibility, which consists primarily in the sheer enumeration of changes and modifications (Jameson, 1991, p x).

As if in exemplification of this, Giddens explores the terminological uncertainty, and concludes that the social condition within which we operate may perhaps be better described as late modern, a term which we would, in the main, endorse. He comments:

> It has become commonplace to claim that modernity fragments, dissociates. Some have even presumed that such fragmentation marks the emergence of a novel phase of social development beyond modernity — a postmodern era. Yet the unifying features of modern institutions are just as central to modernity, especially in the phase of high modernity — as the desegregating ones. ... Taken overall, the many diverse modes of culture and consciousness characteristic of pre-modern 'world systems', formed a genuinely fragmented array of social communities. By contrast, late modernity produces a situation in which humankind in some respects becomes a 'we', facing problems and opportunities where there are no 'others' (Giddens, 1991, p.27).

The theme of this book is thus partly the exploration of the educational consequences of there being no 'others'. It concentrates on the diversity of the population of Europe and the ways in which the diverse groups of children and young people are educated in the schools and universities of Europe. The book attempts to use theories about the nature of late modernity, postmodernity and associated concepts and modes of analysis, to examine how European education systems appear to reproduce, eliminate and exploit diversity. It does this in an eclectic manner, echoing Simon Sharma's view that

> Shameless eclecticism has been my only methodological guide. The thieving magpie approach to other disciplines may seem, superficially, to be new fangled but it is very old fashioned (Sharma, 1991, p.8).

In this spirit, the book utilises the notions associated with debates about late modernity and postmodernity from a range of academic disciplines in order to examine their purchase on contemporary issues within education. It does this without necessarily wishing to announce 'a novel phase of social development', agreeing with Derrida that we are not in the midst of an absolute break with the past:

> I do not believe in decisive ruptures, in an unequivocal 'epistemological break' as it is called today. Breaks are always, and fatally, reinscribed in an old cloth that must continually, interminably be undone. This interminability is not an accident or contingency; it is essential, systematic, and theoretical. And this in no way minimises the necessary

and relative importance of certain breaks, of the appearance and definition of new structures (Derrida, 1972, p.24).

Thus, the authors would wish to assert not that suddenly one day in the early 1970s, we, and European education systems, passed inadvertently from modernity to postmodernity, but rather that the concepts and modes of analysis associated with the identification of modernity, late modernity and postmodernity are exceedingly helpful in understanding many significant issues in European education, particularly those concerned with cultural diversity.

Postmodernity has shifted from being a way of describing cultural products (allusive, disjointed, pastiche, merging subjectivities and so on) to a way of describing society (fractured, relative, pluralistic, gendered and so on). It has also been linked to shifts in the mode of capitalist production often referred to as post-Fordist or post-Taylorist (highly specified, small batch production, niche marketing, just-in-time deliveries, non unionised, deskilled and flexible workforce and so on). The authors are happy to admire those writers who can continue to discern links between the mode of production and the nature of cultural activity and output as the frequent references to, say, Castells and Zukin make clear. However, in the case of education, theoretically desirable as such symmetry may be, in practice it is not easy to discover. It would be pleasing to link changes in the workplace to corresponding changes in school and university practice and curricula; to see educational institutions as mediating changes in the mode of production to changes in cultural forms. Perhaps such links are yet to be made but they remain beyond the scope of this book.

In clarifying this at the outset, it may be that the book is left open to the charge of being 'culturalist' in that it discusses the cultures of Europe and the curricula of schools and universities as if they were separate and distinct from the economic 'base'. Certainly Zukin (1988; 1991), Castells (1989) and, to a lesser extent King (1990a; 1990b; 1990c) have been able to maintain the discourse of base and superstructure, albeit in revisionist terms, beyond the destruction of the Berlin Wall. But they achieve this by insisting on intellectual production, in Castells' case, information technology and in that of Zukin and King, artistic, architectural or gastronomic creations, as an aspect of the economic 'base'. Andy Green also notes the post-Fordist tendency 'towards the substitution of manufacturing industry by new

3

service industries and the replacement of knowledge and expertise for capital as the central variables of modern society' (Green, 1994, p.69). Seen from this perspective the base/superstructure dichotomy is meaningless in an economy which has shifted from capitalism to knowledgism. Strangely, this argument has rarely been applied to educational institutions in this context, although they would seem to be obvious examples.

Knowledge and information are now commodities; amongst the most important and valuable commodities in world trade. Despite the fact that the physical location of knowledge is becoming increasingly difficult to identify (within, say, Internet), schools and universities are, with research institutes, government departments and intergovernmental organisations, the most important sites of the production and exchange of these vital commodities. The links between university research, whether individual or commissioned, and professional application in law, medicine or education are taken for granted. Similarly, links between university research and technical development in industrial application, especially in such areas as pharmaceuticals and armaments, show the economic importance of knowledge production. Pupils and students from countries beyond the European Union, taking courses at schools and universities within the Union are a further manifestation of curricula as export products. In wider terms, popular music, films and television networks and programmes, books and magazines, computer games and software, even religious movements are pre-eminent among the (often highly lucrative) exports of the European Union and, of course, the USA. There is a symbiosis of consumerism between these cultural products and the more obviously industrial products — clothes, toys, sound systems, television, telephone and computer technology — which is mutually supportive both in terms of production and of export. The creation, application and dissemination of these products and technologies, in their turn require further educational developments, from courses on fashion through to those on parallel computing.

It follows then, that neither educational institutions nor culture can any longer be separated (if they ever could) from the economic base. From commercial classes in English or windsurfing, through to the industrial research activities of the universities of Stuttgart and Warwick, educational institutions are a fundamental part of the economic base. Cultural activity,

4

from leisure and tourism through to using sophisticated software are similarly fundamental elements in economic production and consumption. Base-superstructure analysis is one of the achievements of high modernism which cannot withstand, in an unmodified form, either the insights of theories of posmodernity or the changed circumstances of the knowledgist international economy.

Whilst, unlike Usher and Edwards, the authors have not discerned in the literature any helpful distinction between the terms postmodernism and postmodernity and this book uses the two interchangeably, there is a more tangible difference between the language of postmodernity and that of late modernity. Our hesitation over the term postmodern is not only associated with reluctance to announce a dramatic disjuncture in human history, it also indicates a caution lest we be seen as advocates of the postmodern in education; as chic postmodernists. The point about postmodernism is that it attempts to announce the end of great programmes, of grand narratives (Lyotard, 1984). It can hardly then be established as a replacement programme in its own right in education or anywhere else. The opposition between postmodernism and modernity then is not a conflict such as that between Marxism and capitalism. Postmodernity is not a an alternative to modernism. It is rather a sequence of critiques of it. These critiques themselves take various forms:

> To talk about postmodernity, postmodernism or the postmodern is not therefore to designate some fixed and systematic 'thing'. Rather it is to use a loose umbrella term under whose broad cover can be encompassed at one and the same time a condition, a set of practices, a cultural discourse, an attitude and a mode of analysis (Usher and Edwards, 1994, p.7).

Furthermore, to the extent that postmodernity is embodied in written texts, as differentiated from buildings, say, or films, these are frequently presented in language and modes of argumentation which makes them both difficult fully to comprehend and vague and allusive in their final formulations. This difficulty and allusiveness is deliberate: again postmodernist writers rarely allow themselves to be caught in the trap of the definite, the programmatic or the certain which they associate with modernity. However, this book has been written not as a critique of the concept of postmodernity, though certainly some of its limitations are explored, but rather as an investigation

emerging states of Europe thus reflected deeper sets of potentially conflictual pluralities, constantly changing, like political alliances, through time.

This pluralism was often unobserved. When it was noticed, it was frequently suppressed, so that a dominant view of Europe and its place in the world gradually came into place. One consequence of this was that by 1900, many middle class, white, male citizens of France, Germany or the UK would have looked out on the world with an air of benevolent satisfaction. School textbooks would have reflected such satisfaction as well. Scientists had explained the atom and the universe, medical doctors could see their way to curing most illness, sociologists were beginning to claim that they perceived the inner workings of society and psychologists' the inner workings of the human mind and personality. In the background, Christianity dominated the religious world. The power bloc rivals of 1500 had either been colonised or were emerging from the shadow of old fashioned autocratic regimes into the sunshine of modern western style democracy. Apart from colonial wars and the occasional short inter-state war like the Franco-Prussian War of 1870, the European land mass had been ostensibly at peace since 1815.

Some one hundred years later, much of that optimism, albeit optimism located in a small but powerful group, has gone. Indeed, the very description at the start of the previous paragraph is indicative of this change. Even thirty years ago, the phrase 'a European looking out upon the world' would have appeared sufficiently accurate in both intellectual discourse and in school textbooks. A growing awareness of the hegemonic nature of such a statement has been a significant feature of changes in the use of the English language in intellectual discourse and school textbooks over the last two decades (Dunant, 1994). And that world, or rather the perceptions of it, has changed. Scientists in a post-Einstein world wrestle with chaos theory, particle physics and explanations of what happened at the beginning of the universe: they also worry about the devils that they may have unleashed in a post-Hiroshima and gene-manipulating world (Gleick, 1987; Overbye, 1991; Rhodes, 1987). Medical doctors, despite the euphoria following the introduction of drugs like penicillin and the defeat of epidemic diseases such as smallpox, contemplate the search for a cure for HIV/AIDS with increasing gloom. Sociologists contemplate the exhaustion of Marxist and post-Marxist formulations in front of a diminishing audience while psychologists, perhaps the least perturbed, too often see their work perceived as a form of secular confessional. Christianity is, in its mainstream manifestations, still polite: however, globally, religious fundamentalism, particularly Christian and Islamic fundamentalism, offer appealing alternatives to the modern, rational agenda (Kepel, 1993). Perhaps most depressingly, we live in the shadow of the Holocaust and the two major European civil wars of 1914-18 and 1939-45, the latter of which developed into a global conflict that all but finally exhausted Europe.

This unease is, however, not an exclusively modern phenomenon and terms like postmodern and late modern may sometimes disguise and confuse rather than clarify. Behind this book there is a familiar set of educational questions: what should be taught? by whom? to whom? and who should determine this? In the past, such debates in Europe, as in many other parts of the world, have tended to concentrate on issues concerning the relationship of religion and/or class to educational provision, with perhaps a more recent emphasis on the impact of gender and ethnic difference. The attempts by education systems equitably to tackle issues of difference have tended to rest upon one of two assumptions: either that there is an educational answer to these issues, in technical or administrative terms, if only it could be found; or that there is an answer, but that dominating (and usually oppressive) forces within society prevent an identified solution from being put into practice. The latter perspective has, at one time or another, been held by both left- and right-wing contributors to the education debate (the present authors included). In other words, although pluralistic educational approaches have been advocated and implemented, they have been considered within an educational world view of a one best system.

This book attempts to argue something slightly different from a technically un-perfected or politically impossible total educational solution. It starts from the position that the modern or Enlightenment agenda, in education as elsewhere, is more a product of Europe's fractured and contested origins and current status, rather than some universal, uncontested and perfectible project. If this is correct, postmodernity, as Giddens (above) suggests, is not really new but is no more than the latest expression of Europe's contradictions. It is another aspect of understanding that the modern, rational Enlightenment agenda has to be placed in an intellectual

9

framework that recognises the complexities and unpredictable nature of society without turning to fundamentalist and simplistic solutions based in old religions or in free market economics.

This retreat from rationality is not just a contemporary phenomenon. It is part of a long history of conflict between hegemonising and fissile tendencies within Europe, accentuated by the creation of states and their supportive mass education systems. Thus, in order to understand the dilemmas that face contemporary European education systems, it is essential to acknowledge that the issues are neither new nor necessarily intractable, although they may well be peculiarly part of the European heritage.

To understand these issues better, a number of key issues invite initial investigation. They include issues of differentiation and segregation, of the knowledge that schools and universities legitimate and the exact nature of the arena, ('Europe') and the parties ('Europeans') concerned. These investigations cannot readily be ordered in a neat sequential hierarchy of explanation. This book has a theme: European education and cultural diversity, of which the chapters are a set of variations. It is hoped that, by the end of the book, the variations will have helped the reader to a different and better understanding of the theme. Finally, because we are UK Europeans (and male and white), we bring to the task our own sets of knowledge and prejudices, which we have tried to make explicit rather than implicit.

Chapter Two

CLASS, 'RACE' AND EDUCATIONAL ACHIEVEMENT

2.1. Xenophobia in a Uniting Europe

The collapse of European style communism that took place so rapidly during and after 1989, seemed to presage a new age for Europe. Many, in politics and education alike, saw that the earlier optimisms of the Treaty of Rome could be extended into an expanded community, with an increasingly integrated polity based on an enthusiastic endorsement of the Maastricht Treaty. Although education had been deliberately excluded from the original Treaty of Rome, Maastricht, it was hoped, marked a beginning of a greater central provision of education in the individual states of a new, more integrated Union. In particular, the generally poor educational provision for minorities and the continued poor performance of working class children in most of the individual states of the European Union could be tackled from a broader European perspective that eschewed narrow nationalisms and avoided the narrow perspectives on working class education that prevailed in certain member states. Education would then be able to play a significant role in the deepening of the ties of the Union and of its widening northward and eastward.

Much of that earlier optimism has already evaporated. Before the Berlin Wall could be broken down and made into souvenir paperweights, the sheer size of the task of integration of East and West Germany was shaking the new, West-dominated German economy. Teachers in the schools of the new Germany, who had recently been celebrating reunification, found that they faced the issue of nascent fascism in their classrooms as well as in the streets of the communities in which they worked and lived (Dorn, 1993).

Academics in the universities of the old DDR found themselves facing an ideological and stigmatising trial as they attempted to 're-apply' for their posts. German schools and universities were not alone in facing such issues. In 1994, a report on racism in Europe claimed that, despite the fact that much racial violence is not so described by official statistics, the general trend remained upward. Across the European Union, for example, seventy-five racist murders were reported in 1993, as against sixty-six in 1992, a rise of thirteen per cent. In Germany alone, there was a rise from twenty-five murders to fifty-two. Most sadly, seventeen of these racist murders were of school children aged under fifteen (CARF, 1994).

In addition, throughout much of the rest of the former Eastern Europe, education systems were, on the surface at least, turned upside down as the tenets of Marxist-Leninism were replaced overnight by free market economics, nationalism and in some cases, excessive religiosity. In Hungary for example, four curriculum reforms had been proposed between 1989 and 1992, with little hope that even the fourth would be accepted (Szabio, 1993). As well as educational confusion, these schooling systems, like those in former Western Europe, also had to deal with racism and xenophobia, often in national contexts which were ominously silent on the condition of some minorities. Bridge (1993) describes how states like Romania, in addition to making definitions of groups which ignored the significant presence of Gypsies also tacitly ignored direct persecution. Thus, some two million Gypsies became 470,000 in official statistics, their high unemployment rate (seventy eight per cent) was seldom a matter for concern, and when persecution boiled over into murder, official responses were muted. In such a climate, possibilities of ethnic cleansing are all too easy. Bridge reports on one such recent case, where ethnic Romanians are quoted as saying:

> We are proud of what we did. On reflection, though, it would have been better if we had burnt more of the people, not just the houses (Bridge, 1993, p.13).

and

> We did not commit murder — how could you call killing Gypsies murder? Gypsies are not really people, you see. They are always killing each other. They are criminals, sub-human, vermin. And they are certainly not wanted here (p.13).

Although this example is extreme, it is symptomatic of a wider malaise. In the European Union and elsewhere in Europe, education systems continue to face both overt and covert expressions of such xenophobia, often fuelled by economic decline.

Xenophobia is not only a danger in relationships between states. It is at least as much a hazard within states. This becomes even clearer if the global, rather than the European, context is considered.

> In the last three years we have had 82 conflicts — defining conflicts as ones in which more than 1,000 lives were lost. And out of those 82 conflicts, 79 were within nations and only three between nations. These are conflicts between people and ethnic groups rather than between countries (Mahbub ul-Haq, 1994, p. 20).

Chechenia has recently been added to the long catalogue of Europe's within-state conflicts.

2.2. Educational Systems and Differential Achievement

As long-term and enduring as the phenomenon of xenophobia, is the seemingly continual educational underachievement of clearly identifiable groups in the education systems of most European states. What perhaps is new is that the familiar progressive educational policy aspirations, most often based on class inequalities, now seem in need of considerable revision and amplification if they are to be a basis for a more satisfactory educational intervention. However, if some of the earlier explanations seem to have proved inadequate, the issues that they sought to address, in the main, still exist. Central to any discussion of the educational policies associated with these debates has to be the issue of achievement (Jencks, 1972; Mortimore and Blackstone, 1982; Department of Education and Science, 1984). What do many of the children coming from such disadvantaged groups actually achieve in the schools of Europe?

The precise usage of achievement needs to be made clear. Common measures of educational achievement include literacy and numeracy levels, drop-out and repetition rates, public examination results, access to secondary and tertiary education and successful entry to the job market. There are other, less easily measured achievements too, such as tolerance and the acquisition of sets of values that eschew racism, xenophobia, sexism and other forms of discriminatory behaviour and belief. At the same time, it has to be acknowledged that educational achievement, of whatever sort, is usually differentially distributed, with some students being more 'successful' than other students. Even where criterion referencing rather than norm referencing is the measure of the achievement or attainment, pupils and students will still achieve at different levels.

Measuring the individual achievement levels of students is relatively uncomplicated. In the main, such variation is both accepted and expected. Measuring the individual achievement levels of *groups* of students is, however, a much more complex task. The groupings and variations most frequently examined in educational contexts are variations in achievement levels between girls and boys, between working class and middle class students and between differing minority groups, often defined in ethnic or 'racial' terms. ('Racial' is placed in inverted commas to indicate its problematic nature. Human 'races' have no basis in contemporary biology but clearly have social science significance (Tierney, 1982).) Such analyses of the educational achievements of different groups of pupils reveal very complex patterns of educational performance. Most frequently, but not axiomatically, socially and/or economically disadvantaged groups have low levels of educational achievement, whether norm or criterion referenced, particularly if the achievements measured are related to formal school knowledge and its assessment.

Such low levels of performance indicate, at the initial level of analysis, that to the social and/or economic disadvantage suffered by many minority and other groups has to be added a further disadvantage, namely educational disadvantage. This in turn feeds on and sustains the two larger forms of disadvantage. This is because of the power of education in terms of its role in vocational and academic selection through qualifications and credentials. Thus low levels of educational achievement by a particular minority or other disadvantaged group help to ensure their continued marginalisation. However, as was indicated earlier, such under- achievement has many forms and many causes.

The most obvious concern in relation to forms of underachievement is in terms of academic achievement which is most commonly expressed in terms of public/national examination results. Many minority and other disadvantaged group students do badly in such examinations, or do not enter for them at all, either having dropped out of schooling prior to the

14

examination year or years, or having been locked into patterns of class repetition that have meant their reaching statutory leaving age well before they have entered the examination class year. If they take the examinations, they frequently do badly in them, confirming their disadvantage and in some circumstances, confirming those negative stereotypes of their educational potential held by society in general and some of their teachers in particular. Such failure in relation to public examinations often has immediate impact on subsequent life chances, reproducing the disadvantaged position of the group in question as well as ensuring that of the individual student.

There are other forms of underachievement. Disadvantaged groups tend to drop out of school earlier and in disproportionate numbers, again perpetuating disadvantage and also discontent. Saying this is not to re-assert a direct link between economic growth and educational investment. Such a link is far from proved. As Massimo Paci put it, referring specifically to Italy, but claiming a more general significance,

> ...we do not today possess a satisfactory theory on the relationship between the development of education and the evolution of the economic system's labour demand (Paci, 1977, p.340).

However, educational investment in relation to disadvantaged groups probably does have some significance, the more so if the groups in question are currently economically marginalised, although the power of education in this regard should never be exaggerated. Lester Thurow's classic attack on simplistic education investment policies is a useful counterpoint here, particularly his argument that:

> ...our reliance on education as the ultimate public policy for curing all problems, economic and social, is unwarranted at best, and in all probability ineffective (Thurow, 1977, p.335).

If the link between education, economic development and greater equality of opportunity is not as strong as some in education might desire, it is, however, still present. It is certainly more tangible than the consequences of an inadequate education on such children's spiritual, cultural, aesthetic and moral development. It is a powerfully held belief of educators that education has a significant contribution to make in these areas of a young person's development. How it is effected and how it is measured are much more difficult issues. What may be asserted here, however, is that many

European schooling systems do little for these areas of growth in relation to minorities and may often produce curricular offerings that oppose, ignore or disparage those crucial aspects of the child's background.

2.3. Curricular Systems and Differential Attainment

The factors that are at work in relation to these issues in European education systems' failure to meet the needs of many groups of minority and other disadvantaged groups of children and young people are varied. Amongst the most significant are inadequate educational policies and funding and inappropriate curricula. The nature of the curricular offerings and the subsequent learning that takes place is again based on individual state views of the knowledge, skills and information that students should possess. The issues raised by the curriculum in relation to minorities and other disadvantaged groups make an already difficult area highly complex. Most states provide broad guidelines within which education systems operationalise provision in relation to such groups. Interestingly, the educational issues are not, in the first instance, resource driven. In other words, much more could be done to meet these groups' needs and aspirations more adequately within the school curriculum without an input of expensive extra resources.

What is required initially is an answer to a seeming contradictory set of propositions. The first is that the educational system has a responsibility to help produce a loyal and unified citizenry. To do this, the curriculum should avoid the accentuation of difference. The dissatisfaction to which this may give rise may well itself endanger the unity of the state. The second is that the education system, by supporting and encouraging linguistic, religious, historical and other differences may well endanger the unity of the state. In other words, whatever decisions are made they may well cause difficulties in terms of state unity.

There are at least two ways of resolving this paradox. The first is that each state education system has to make decisions based on its current inclination. The second is that state education systems must recognise the essentially contested nature of their enterprise and neither seek nor expect consensus on curricular issues within an intercultural education system. Both these positions consciously reject relativism but do assert that, in view

such unrepresentative curricula is not always easy to specify. Suppressing such partial and xenophobic histories within a school history curriculum is not enough. Indeed, suppression is seldom effective: such narrow, communalistic histories have to be constantly challenged. For example, the current rise of anti-semitism, fascism and racism across Europe may show how unsuccessful the education system has been in teaching about Europe's past. On the other hand, it must also be stated clearly that things could be a good deal worse if it had not been for the efforts made in schools, colleges and other educational institutions across Europe to combat anti-semitism and racism.

Despite that caveat, it would seem that the Holocaust, perhaps the key to an understanding of contemporary Europe, is still not given the curricular space and treatment that it deserves. But other examples abound. Clearly, the teaching of history in the former states of Yugoslavia failed to give many people the skills with which to deal with the rise of ethnic particularism. Indeed, in respect of this, the response of many within Europe (and elsewhere) to the Muslim/Christian violence has been one of puzzlement about the presence and long standing survival of Islam within Europe, a story that is taken up later in Chapter Four. Similar examples could, sadly, be readily drawn from all around the world.

Although schools and universities may appear to be insignificant in relation to these powerful xenophobic forces, it is surely correct that educational institutions should constantly, in the history curriculum and elsewhere, give children alternative histories that challenge such nationalisms and xenophobia. In other words, the curriculum can include, exclude or ignore groups who are citizens of the state and whose children attend school within it. But it excludes them at a cost. An intercultural curriculum, on the other hand, that is including of groups rather than excluding of them, is potentially a source of a much more effective, appropriate and successful education for all students.

The teaching of history is but part of a systematic and sustained approach to providing an effective education within the modern, pluralistic state. This book is not just putting forward a postmodern agenda for combating racism and xenophobia within schools and the wider society, it is also arguing that the modern agenda is not discredited but should be seen as more complex than has hitherto been the case. As Arnowitz and Giroux put it:

Modernism is far from dead — its central categories are simply being written within a plurality of narratives that are attempting to address the new set of social, political, technical and scientific configurations that constitute the current age (Arnowitz and Giroux, 1991, p.63).

Such plurality of narratives make it difficult for policy makers in general and educational policy makers in particular, to plan. The need for an intercultural education policy and practice remains contested in most European state education systems. Plurality and complexity have been constant but unrecognised features of European states for a long period of time; it has now become an urgent task for education systems to respond to these circumstances.

Chapter Three

MODERNIST KNOWLEDGE AND NATIONAL CURRICULUM SYSTEMS

3.1. Modernist Knowledge

The curricular issues identified towards the end of the previous chapter rest upon the assumption that there is a connection between the epistemology current in a particular society and the content of the school and higher education curriculum within it. In the case of those countries where the curriculum of schools and/or higher education institutions is determined by the government, this connection is likely to be through the political process. The more detailed the state control of educational knowledge, the more openly political is likely to be the nature of the determination. Where there is detailed and politicised determination of the curriculum — as is frequently the case with regard to say, the History curriculum — the epistemology may well be contested in political terms. It is likely, however, that there will be limits to these epistemological contests since even opposed political perspectives in a given society are likely to share many assumptions about the nature of human knowledge.

This is partly because any curriculum, at the level of school or even university, can only be a small selection from what humanity knows or claims to know. This process of selection has at least three stages. The first stage will be how knowledge is organised. At school level almost all European countries choose — and the point is that this is a choice — to organise curricular knowledge in the form of subjects, or, at a more abstruse level, in the form of readily identifiable and distinct cognitive structures.

This organisation was most challengingly advocated by Paul Hirst in the late 1960s and 1970s when he claimed:

...the development of human mind has been marked by the progressive differentiation of human consciousness of some seven or eight distinguishable cognitive structures, each of which involves the making of a distinctive form of reasoned judgement and is therefore, a unique expression of man's (sic) rationality. This is to say that all knowledge and understanding is logically locatable within a number of domains, within, I suggest, mathematics, the physical sciences, the human sciences and history, literature and the fine arts, morals, religion and philosophy (Hirst, 1975, p.294).

Such a view is not just powerful in schools. At the higher education level, this remains the preferred organisation of knowledge, although new joint honours, modular programmes and professional studies may be starting to break down the traditional pattern. So hegemonic is the epistemology of subject disciplines that for many graduates and academics it is the only way they can perceive human knowledge to be organised. A glance at the mix and match system of modularisation on offer in some North American universities or, for that matter, at the topic approach in English primary schools; rapidly being displaced by the National Curriculum, would dispel this beguiling and reassuring sense of epistemological monism. Equally, it ignores forms of schooling found throughout Europe that are based on clear alternatives, such as the supplementary Qu'ranic schools found within many cities of the European Union.

The second process of selection, in the discipline-based approach to curriculum planning, is which subjects will actually be taught at which levels of education. Again for many lecturers, teachers and pupils, the subjects selected by a specific country appear to be the only possible, sensible school or university curriculum. Few academics would dispute that mathematics, science and the national language(s) should be taught to all pupils. However, what these curricular labels refer to is not so clear cut. More, within Europe there is less agreement about at what age this self-evident curriculum should start or finish. Beyond these issues, too often seen as non-problematic, differences will increase with regard to how much technology or history or music children should be compelled to learn and to what level and age. Less traditional subjects such as the social sciences, non-European and minority languages or those such as classics with a waning vocational appeal, are at the fringes of the curriculum in many European countries. Their inclusion and development is subject to political exigency or the preferences and skills of individual headteachers and teachers.

The third process of selection in the discipline-based paradigm, concerns the issue briefly referred to in the previous paragraph, namely, what is to constitute school and university knowledge within any particular favoured subject? Which aspects of atomic theory or exegesis of Schiller, Shakespeare, Cervantes or Dante do politicians and professionals consider it necessary for pupils and students to learn? Also controversial are which periods and/or topics of the history of the world, of Europe, of the specific country are to be taught to the next generation of citizens. And, as was noted in the previous chapter, there is an increasing debate over which other languages should be taught and which should be compulsory. Related to all these, and of course many similar issues, is the age at which such learning should start or finish. Behind the decisions that are made on all of these, most frequently by examination authorities as well as by politicians and professionals, there are judgements or implicit assumptions about the nature and value of both knowledge and culture.

Perhaps knowledge more than any other ideal lies at the heart of the Enlightenment project (Lyotard, 1984). The Enlightenment was a product of the expansion of knowledge. It was also a statement of faith in knowledge both as a way of understanding truth and as the essential instrument in ensuring human progress. In their illuminating discussion of Derrida, Usher and Edwards provide a sound account of the centrality of teaching and education to the Enlightenment project:

> ... Bauman ... refers to Spinoza's dictum that ' if I know the truth and you are ignorant, to make you change your thoughts and ways is my moral duty; refraining from doing so would be cruel and selfish'. Bauman argues that it is this notion of *necessity* to educate, of education's historical role to enlighten and emancipate, which is at the very heart of the project of modernity. ... education is itself a historically located cultural construct, constructed through a narrative which is not simply a means of understanding the world but also of continually

changing it through the attempt to mould the subjectivities of those within it (Usher and Edwards, 1994, p.125).

It is interesting to note that this faith in knowledge is still held by mainstream modernists: thus Gellner can write in his book *Postmodernism, Reason and Religion*:

> When dealing with serious matters, when human lives and welfare are at stake, when major resources are being committed, the only kind of knowledge which may legitimately be used and invoked is that which satisfies the criteria of Enlightenment philosophy — notwithstanding the fact that it is not easy to formulate these with precision or to general satisfaction, and that it may be impossible to demonstrate their authority (Gellner 1992, p. 92).

Much of this chapter is concerned with the nature of this modernist knowledge and its relationship to national or regional curriculum systems. The National Curriculum in England and Wales is currently the most state controlled in the European Union: it is used as a brief example in this chapter. However, at the outset, it is appropriate to stress not merely the nature of this modernist knowledge but its availability and accessibility. One of the Enlightenment ideals was that knowledge should be much more generally, in some views universally, available. Hence, the institutions of universal schooling are themselves — with hospitals, asylums, prisons and public libraries and galleries — among the major legacies of the Enlightenment: an area perhaps most challengingly explored by Foucault (Foucault, 1967; 1970; 1972; 1973; 1979).

Enlightenment thinkers believed in the power of their knowledge and that societies would inevitably be improved, though not necessarily made more democratic, the wider this power was disseminated. Schools and universities would improve the quality of individual human lives and simultaneously the prosperity and well being of societies. Again it is not being suggested that these beliefs are historically limited to the eighteenth or nineteenth century: they form part of the conscious ideology of many of those people involved in the running and working of education systems in Europe today. Despite the claims of some of those advocating a postmodern education agenda, the Enlightenment project in education is far from exhausted:

It may be that the old orthodoxies of Enlightenment progressivism suppressed heterogeneity and difference but it is hard to see how any project of political emancipation can proceed without drawing upon their traditions of critical thought and practice (Carter, 1993, pp.154-155).

The use of postmodernity and late modernity in the following chapters is to highlight changes within the Enlightenment programme rather than to indicate its absolute curtailment. Modernity might have succeeded traditionalism, though it eradicated less of its legacy than its proponents might have imagined. Similarly, as modernity itself begins to collapse (Chapter Five) a plurality of perspectives emerges which includes the revised traditionalist as well as the formulations of late and postmodernity.

Academic knowledge is both a major origin and a major strand of the entire Enlightenment project. It is not, despite the protagonists of modernism, the only strand: industrial capitalism, nationalism and the institutionalisation of social control in terms of both gender and class relations form some of its other and more questionable themes. The effect of the development of late seventeenth century science and philosophy, exemplified by, say, Newton's *Summa Mathematica*, was to open up possibilities for the human mind which even the Renaissance had never envisaged (Munck, 1990). Humanity was now not only the measure of all things, it was able to understand and codify with astonishing exactitude and predictability the orderings of the universe itself. It seemed clear that nothing could be beyond human understanding, that nothing was prohibited to human research, that everything was susceptible to human control. Alongside the Renaissance belief in the goodness and beauty of truth, the Enlightenment discovered the power of knowledge. There has been, as yet, no Counter Reformation for the Enlightenment Project, although it could be argued that elements of the Romantic Movement may have come close to it. The Industrial Revolution in the towns of Northern England and the political Revolutions in the American colonies and Paris swept the Enlightenment Project into seemingly uncontested global prominence. From Summa Mathematica to Los Alamos, human knowledge appeared to offer infinite power and control.

For, of course, it is science which lies at the centre of modernist knowledge: science as a form of classification (Linnaeus), as a record of heroic discoveries (*The Origin of Species*) and as a method of achieving truth (Popper, 1966a; 1966b; 1972). More even than this, the Enlightenment saw science as a way of improving the human condition. Among the many products of this belief in the efficacy of scientific knowledge are medicine, public health, industrialisation and the concomitant rise in state-funded technical and scientific education. To be clear about our own emphasis here, the effects of modernist knowledge, and of the belief in science in particular, have not been unambiguously beneficial. Enlightenment science perceives nature as something to be explored, classified, experimented with, exploited and dominated. The forthcoming ecological crisis is one of the achievements of the Enlightenment programme. One of the triumphs of education systems as modes of implementation of modernity is that it is still Enlightenment science which is taught in European schools and universities and not those alternative sciences which might belatedly prevent or at least mitigate this crisis (Orr 1992; 1993). (This issue is discussed in more detail in Chapter Seven.) But before moving to a further consideration of science, it is necessary to consider two further aspects of modernist knowledge, those concerned with social sciences and those concerned with culture.

The social sciences are effectively a product of modernism. The application of academic, preferably scientific, knowledge to individual and social human conditions and difficulties effectively begins in the Enlightenment. Adam Smith, Bentham, Compte, Durkheim and Binet, even Marx, demonstrate that systematic analysis of social and individual data can reveal both knowledge about the human condition and possible strategies for ameliorating it. Modernist social science emphasised the importance of data collection, even data construction; the application of social and individual data to practical circumstances; the establishment of a canon of revered authorities. Almost as much as through science and geology, it was through the social sciences that modernism most clearly distanced itself from religion. Heroic social science investigators such as Booth preceded the sociological attack on individual autonomy and action. By the time Durkheim was formulating this critical discourse, the cult of narcissistic individualism was already being propagated by Freud and his followers. The politics of self determination of individual 'rights' and the economics of the consumer vote and individual choice combined into an overarching modernist social science which stressed individuality, the ability of human beings to control their own circumstances, the responsibility of government to respond to and reflect the multitude of individual preferences without in any way infringing the 'rights' and liberty of the citizens. Structuralist sociology — whether of Marx or of Durkheim — provided the only dissident voice.

In terms of culture, the establishment of canons, whether national or European, cannot be laid exclusively at the door of the Enlightenment. Renaissance Florentine scholars, such as Ficino, were concerned both with the re-discovery of the ancient canon and with the establishment of a modern vernacular equivalent (Cronin, 1992a; 1992b). This duality held sway throughout Europe until comparatively recently. An elite educated European had a familiarity with a classical literary canon that crossed state frontiers. Classical Greek and Latin writers and the Bible were at its core, followed by a further list of the great and good of European literature, writers such as Dante, Shakespeare, Cervantes, Milton, Goethe and Ibsen. Their importance was stressed, and the canon maintained and reproduced, in the education systems of Europe, especially in the universities. The way in which this duality was intensified and partially polarised was reflected in the widening curriculum of the expanding university sector in the nineteenth century and in the emergence of the academic study of the vernacular canon. How this emergence relates to the contemporaneous burgeoning of nationalism is not too clear, although in some of its exponents, such as Sir Arthur Quiller-Couch, the links are made explicit. In Pick's excellent account (1993), he quotes at length some of the more extreme views that were put forward to justify the teaching of English, such as Basil Willy's statement that a separate English degree meant that '...students and lovers of our literature could pursue their chosen subject without having to endure the alien yoke of Teutonic philology' (quoted in Pick, 1993, p.139).

Quiller-Couch went further, arguing that 'noble weapon of English, testing its poise and edge', was a language to be safeguarded and protected from perverse Teutonic influences (p. 139). Such statements seem almost measured when laid against some of the more extreme comments that Pick unearthed, such as that made by Spencer Warren in 1914:

> The Germans today have somehow got it into their heads that they are, before all other nations, a nation of poets. Can they compare with us?

Let us put it into naval language. Their 'Grand Fleet' seems somewhat limited. Grant that they have one 'super Dreadnought, the 'Goethe', admittedly a fine and powerful ship; still, she is hardly equal in guns or speed to the 'Shakespeare' (Pick, 1993, p.147).

Such views are, admittedly, extreme. However they demonstrate that there was a clear link between the national literary canon, its study and nationalism, a little of which still remains, albeit in more muted forms.

The establishment of the literature canon produced a tradition. In England, this tradition building was not confined to F. R. Leavis (1962; 1963; 1964): Ezra Pound (1938; 1960) and T. S.Eliot (1955) had similarly engaged themselves in the inter-war period. And they in turn were part of a longer tradition, in which the work of Johnson and Arnold was particularly influential. In a modified form, such views have persisted. University English departments in England (and the same argument could be made for other countries, certainly France) had by 1960 established at least two principles to their own satisfaction, which some still attempt to maintain. These were the superiority of the English literary canon over any other ancient or modern and the tightly controlled criteria whereby that canon could be elaborated (Batsleer, et al,. 1985).

The establishment of such a tradition did not take place in a vacuum. Amongst other things, it involved particular selections and interpretations of history. Since both the canon and the selected traditions were highly influenced by, as well as influential on, the state nationalism which was central to the Enlightenment project, the version of history which emerged was particular to modernism. This is the version of history which invented the notion of a Great European Tradition. It stressed a clear and unquestioned 'heritage' from Ancient Greece, through the Roman Republic and Empire to the Renaissance and thence to the Western European countries of the Enlightenment. These countries were seen as the political, literary and cultural heirs of Ancient Greece. If necessary, in order to sustain this, the history of both Europe and Greece itself could be re-written (see Chapters Four and Seven). Critically, the Tradition was exclusively European. It did not acknowledge or respect cultures or traditions beyond Europe, let alone acknowledge that they might have played a part in the development of the European Tradition. Whilst pan-Europeanism might have modified the nationalism of the modernist project, this only paved the way for the emergence of a wider European nationalism.

This book proposes a classification of European curricular systems as being traditional, modernist or post-modern (see especially Chapter Five). Three aspects of this classification need to be stressed at the outset. Firstly, it is not chronological: in curricular terms all three themes probably exist simultaneously in the countries of the European Union. Secondly, although in wider terms these movements may be seen to be successive, this should not imply any view of progress or even of irreversibility. The triumph of fundamentalist religions is a reminder that traditionalism is by no means dead. Similarly, it is far too early to assert that post-modernism has succeeded modernism. Some (Harvey, 1989) see post-modernism as only a phase in the wider modernist movement. Nor does this book assert that such approaches offer the possibility of curricular utopia, though one of its major themes is that they offer an essential critique to modernist knowledge systems. Thirdly, the classification is pragmatic. It is not an attempt to establish a major epistemological system (though such is the aspiration of many of the authors whom we reference) but rather to offer a terminology in which the conflicts over the curricular systems in the European states and in the European Union itself, can be analysed.

The impact of modernist knowledge on the curriculum of schools and universities has varied quite markedly between countries. Whilst the French curriculum can be seen in modernist terms at least since Napoleonic times, in England and Wales there has always been a tendency towards a more traditionalist curriculum. During the nineteenth century, for instance, the stress on religious education, the concentration on the 3 Rs and the high status which continued to be awarded to the classics would seem to indicate that curricula in schools and universities were successfully resistant to modernism. Technical and scientific education arrived surprisingly late in England and Wales. Similarly, the continued importance of the churches in schools and higher education, as well as revised governmental emphasis on religious education and daily acts of worship in school indicate that the modernist epistemology, never mind any possible successor, has not yet completely overwhelmed the English and Welsh curriculum.

The concept of modernism includes trends which many commentators on the curriculum have seen as being self-contradictory rather than unitary

(Jones, 1989; Coulby and Bash, 1991). Those, such as the former Manpower Services Commission, who stressed vocational relevance, are as much a part of modernist epistemology as those who advocate elitist and ethnocentric teaching of literature and history. However, this does not mean that they will agree on curricular priorities. The modernist system of knowledge was fractured before the self-conscious emergence of postmodernism. Furthermore, not all the strands in current European right-wing thinking on the curriculum can be regarded as modernist, containing as they do, traditionalist and postmodern strands.

3.2. The Collapse of Modernist Knowledge.

Los Alamos was and still is a part of the University of California. The making of the first atomic bombs was both the triumph and also, in some ways, the termination of the Enlightenment project. Through science, the Los Alamos team and the United States had created an unimaginably destructive weapon and had immediately utilised it to end global conflict apparently indefinitely. Academics, scientists, had unquestionably changed the world (Rhodes, 1988). The modern programme had been able to intervene in the affairs of humanity in a way in which Condorcet could never have imagined. Yet this success lay in the creation of a deadly nuclear technology. Modernism had created this technology without the governmental, moral and philosophical apparatus with which to control it. Whilst humanity might be in awe of the final achievement of modernism, it would also be in fear for its survival as a consequence of this new technology. After the destruction of Hiroshima and Nagasaki the benevolence of the Enlightenment project would never again receive unhesitating endorsement. Whilst the rest of this section goes on to list and analyse those critiques which undermined modernist epistemology in the post-war period, the impact of the fearful success of nuclear technology should be seen as a critical blow.

There have been at least three major critiques of modernist knowledge: the feminist critique, the culturalist (sometimes 'race' or ethnicity) critique and the class critique. Whilst at least the latter of these had been well stated a long time before the last world war, it is since then that the three critiques have been generally substantiated in educational terms. It is also in this period that their combined rather than individual weight has been felt.

Finally, it is during this period that these critiques have influenced on the curricula of schools and higher education institutions in Europe (and of course, elsewhere).

It is probably the feminist critique which has had the most devastating effect on modernist knowledge, not least because modernity has often dissociated from itself half of humanity. The feminist critique reveals that history, culture, science and technology are, fallaciously, seen to be the products of men and are so presented within the curricula of schools and universities. The activities of men were (and still are) privileged by many male academics and are confused by them with the activities of the whole of humanity. Academic history is too often the history of what men did, written by men and taught by men (there are still few female academics). Literary and cultural achievements are evaluated by men who privilege the work of men and the domains in which men have chosen to work. The activities and achievements of women were (and frequently remain) hidden, undervalued and negated. Indeed, the very language used is male dominated (Spender, 1980; Cameron, 1985). From this point of view, Modernist knowledge is flawed in at least three ways. Firstly, the canon of knowledge itself is incomplete, since it values disproportionately those areas of activity and research which have been conducted primarily by men. Secondly, the criteria whereby human knowledge is defined, because themselves elaborated and used by men, are biased towards the selection of work produced by men. Thirdly and consequently, within the various areas of knowledge, the selection of material is biased towards that produced by men — did England produce no female seventeenth century poets? Florence no quattrocento female artists?

Parenthetically, it is necessary to stress that a total harmony between postmodernism and feminism cannot be assumed. It has been pointed out that postmodernism seeks to abandon and debunk the grand narratives just at the point at which women had succeeded in establishing such a narrative of their own. In this respect Arnowitz and Giroux quote at length from Nancy Harstock. The quotation is worthy of repetition since it points to some of the conflicts in and limitations of the postmodernist critique.

Somehow it seems highly suspicious that it is at this moment in history, when so many groups are engaged in 'nationalisms' which involve redefinitions of the marginalised Others, that doubt arises in the

33

academy about the nature of the 'subject', about the possibilities for a general theory which can describe the world, about historical 'progress'. Why is it, exactly at the moment when so many of us who have been silenced begin to demand the right to name ourselves, to act as subjects rather than objects of history, that just then the concept of subjecthood becomes 'problematic'? Just when we are forming our own theories about the world, uncertainty emerges about whether the world can be adequately theorised? (Harstock, quoted in Arnowitz and Giroux, 1991, p.79).

The culturalist critique follows the same pattern as that offered by feminism. Modernist knowledge is white, Western knowledge. It is constructed according to what white Western society has seen to be important. It attempts to relegate the knowledge of other cultures to superstition or folkways (Rodney, 1972). It only recognises academic, scientific and cultural achievement within a very few countries — Greece (but not for the last two millennia), Italy, Germany, the Netherlands, the United Kingdom, France and, belatedly, the United States. The activities and achievements of the rest of humanity are effectively ignored, patronised or belittled within modernist knowledge (James, 1963). This connects knowledge to nationalism, another important element in the Enlightenment project. Such modernist knowledge can be chauvinistic and nationalistic as well as Eurocentric. Worst, it has been used to justify the subjugation and enslavement of whole peoples (Baldwin, 1961; Himes, 1973; Robinson, 1983; Williams, 1966).

There are at least three further ways in which this view of knowledge is flawed. Firstly, the canon of knowledge is fundamentally incomplete since it includes mostly those activities and achievements which have derived from Europe. Secondly, the criteria whereby knowledge is defined, because principally elaborated and used by white people, are biased towards the selection of work produced by their own group. Thirdly and consequently, within the various areas of knowledge, the selection of material is biased towards that produced by white people, particularly those from Western Europe. In consequence modernist knowledge is incomplete in a number of major ways. First, it finds it difficult to recognise the knowledge, culture and science generated outside Western Europe and its European offshoots in North America. Secondly, it cannot acknowledge the major contributions to Europe's own knowledge and culture made by other traditions. Finally, it hides from its responsibility for the black diaspora and the worst excesses of slavery and colonialism.

The third major critique is based on class. As suggested above, Marx belonged to the Enlightenment project and was one of its major critics. This is as true of his critique of culture as it is of his dissent from the doctrine of individualism. It is, as ever, worth recalling his commentary on culture in The German Ideology:

> The ideas of the ruling class are in every epoch the ruling ideas, i.e. the class which is the ruling material force of society is at the same time its ruling intellectual force. The class which has the means of material production at its disposal, has control at the same time over the means of mental production ... The ruling ideas are nothing more than the ideal expression of the dominant material relationships, the dominant material relationships grasped as ideas ... (Marx in McLellan (ed) 1977 p. 176).

·It is not necessary to subscribe wholeheartedly to base-superstructure theory (see Chapter One), nor to stick rigidly to the cause of the pre-eminence of the economic to acknowledge the justice of this critique. The tastes of the privileged classes are still too easily reified by academics as preferred artistic, literary or philosophical value systems. The link between elite consumption and art is both an important element in the creation of mass markets and a key to the formation of culture. For Zukin the art museum is an extension of the department store:

> While these processes enhance the role of culture in social differentiation, they also equalise perceptions of cultural production 'for the market' and 'for art'. This is the conundrum of postmodern culture. (Zukin 1991 p.54).

This conundrum is all the more complex when artistic and cultural production, in schools and universities, has become a major element in the industrial profile of many European cities: 'Technological revolutions are made up of innovations whose products are in fact processes' (Castells 1989, p.15). Furthermore, schools and universities are themselves the sites of the marketing and cultural products from postmodern architecture to nouvelle cuisine.

The canons of modernism from Coleridge to Auerbach are, to return to Marx's insight, like the display cabinets in a European country mansion, replete with the old and precious purchases of the super-rich of a previous generation. In UK terms, the canon is now enshrined in the National Curriculum as the mansion is now owned by the National Trust. At the mansion the working class must pay to come and goggle at the possessions of the rich, while, in the school, the National Curriculum attempts to make certain forms of cultural adulation compulsory for all children and young people. The culture of the poor and often even their languages (see Chapter Six) are either neglected or actively suppressed in such national curricular systems. This simultaneously reduces the variety of the curriculum for everybody and alienates a large section of the school (for this component is unlikely to carry on to university) population from what the institution is claiming to offer.

Each of these three critiques of modernist knowledge is powerful in its own way. And of course there are more; for example, new perspectives based upon more open explorations of sexual orientations. Furthermore, the cluster of ideas which centre around Foucault's historical relativism have also played a significant, if less direct and polemic, part in undermining modernist knowledge. Foucault's historical investigation of mental illness, for instance, undermines modernist distinctions between madness and sanity. In exploring this he manages to throw into question the validity of both medical practice and positivist science in general.

If we wanted to analyse the profound structures of objectivity in the knowledge and practice of nineteenth century psychiatry from Pinel to Freud, we should have to show in fact that such objectivity was from the start a reification of a magical nature, which could only be accomplished with the complicity of the patient himself (sic), and beginning from a transparent and clear moral practice, gradually forgotten as positivism imposed its myths of scientific objectivity; a practice forgotten in its origins and its meaning, but always used and always present. What we call psychiatric practice is a certain moral tactic contemporary with the end of the eighteenth century, preserved in the rites of asylum life, and overlaid by the myths of positivism (Foucault, 1967, p.276).

Here, as elsewhere, Foucault looks back at the Enlightenment with a profound scepticism towards its entire modernist project.

When these critiques are taken together they have shaken the faith of some modernists. Postmodernity can be seen as the culmination and the aftermath of these three critiques. Women's knowledge, culture and activity patterns are at least as much a part of this as are the stress on women's rights. Postmodernism has gone beyond cultural relativism and the celebration of the exotic to epistemological relativism. No truth system is seen as being superior. Individual taste and discrimination are encouraged, eclecticism prized and all canons subjected to furious attack. Whilst the title of this section is overstated in suggesting that modernist knowledge has collapsed, it certainly no longer carries any widespread legitimacy. It is too simple to see this as an historical process with modernism gradually being superseded by postmodernism. In terms of knowledge and culture the proponents of each are engaged in a conflict which, in Europe at least, has taken on both a political and educational form, most noticeably in terms of the impact of the market on knowledge choices and subsequent reform of curricula.

3.3. The State Enforcement of Modernist Knowledge

It may seem hard to visualise what a postmodernist school curriculum would look like. But in fact just such a curriculum was in the process of being created in many urban Local Education Authorities in England and Wales prior to the 1988 Education Act. The removal of selection tests at the end of primary education (the 'eleven plus' test) had freed primary schools to engage in curriculum innovation. Whilst the extent of this has often been overstated, many schools had gone some way to eroding modernist subject boundaries through what had become known as the topic approach or the integrated curriculum. Much practice undertaken under this label was perhaps superficial but at its best it was exciting, informative and liberating (Coulby and Ward, 1990). There were other signs of a greater pluralism in the educational provision. Multicultural approaches to knowledge had been adopted by primary and secondary schools, and, with less enthusiasm in higher education, during the 1970s (Cole, 1989). More radically in the 1980s, following the lead of the Inner London Education Authority (ILEA), inner city schools had developed anti-racist and anti-sexist policies (ILEA

1983a; 1983b; 1983c; 1983d; 1983e; 1985). In some cases the resulting curriculum initiatives constituted an attack on modernist knowledge.

It was certainly as an attack that they were understood by the Conservative government, itself wedded to another theory, namely the supremacy of the market, fundamentalist economics. The introduction of a compulsory National Curriculum firmly snatched the initiative back to modernist knowledge. Multiculturalist, anti-racist or anti-sexist analysis was to form no part of an unreconstructed Conservative National Curriculum. If schools and teachers attempted to persist with such programmes, it was in the face of a daily flow of paper from the government, telling them in ever increasing detail what they really ought to be teaching. Since the National Curriculum was so overcrowded and since each school's crucial, because public, test results appeared to depend on the diligence with which it was followed, postmodernist knowledge had effectively been squeezed out of schools in England and Wales, at least up to the point in the early 1990s when teachers' industrial action over time-consuming and inappropriate testing forced a review of the whole edifice. After a series of placatory reviews (Dearing, 1993a; 1993b; DFE 1993a; 1993b), a revised curriculum published in galley proofs in 1994 (*National Curriculum Orders for England*) slimmed down the content but left the essentially modernist structure substantially unaffected.

The state enforcement of modernist and nationalist knowledge at both country and European Union level is a theme throughout this book. What the example of England and Wales shows is three important lessons, two old and one new. Firstly, that curriculum selection is a political issue in which the central state will not hesitate to engage itself. Secondly, that the complexity and relative autonomy of educational institutions is such that even the legal power of the state may not find its definition of knowledge uncontested. Thirdly, and this appears new, that the traditional right and left divisions within a state's educational system are no longer so clearly apparent. For example, the UK 1988 Education Reform Act contains traditional, modern and postmodern aspirations which are actually in conflict. In the same way, opposition to the changes were both reflective of traditional, modern and postmodern perspectives. The potential for unusual new educational alliances is considerable, not just within the UK, but throughout Europe as a whole.

Just as the terms used for analysis of the knowledge used in schools are difficult to clarify, the same is true of other seeming unproblematic concepts. The terms 'Europe' and 'European', central to the concerns of this book, have been used throughout the first three chapters as relatively unproblematic. This is not in fact the case, as the next chapter will seek to demonstrate.

just as the conclusion that . . . .

Chapter Four

THE EDUCATIONAL CONSTRUCTION OF EUROPE

4.1. 'The Reverse of Europe'

The last chapter ended on the state of curriculum debates in today's Europe. This is not a new debate. The introduction of mass schooling in the states of Europe in the nineteenth century was characterised by fierce debates about its purpose and control (Archer, 1984; Green, 1991). Church-state relations, the needs of industry and how these might best be met through schooling, the 'cultivation', 'civilisation' and/or control of the masses and the inculcation and maintenance of patriotism were some of the more important areas that were contested.

What was not really contested and still is not, was a whole series of assumptions about Europe, Europeans and European civilisation. Apart from some polite cultural bows towards certain aspects of ancient Egyptian, Chinese and Indian civilisation and a view that the United States of America was a sort of country cousin to the Great (that is European) Powers, the view was widely held that progress was not only certain but that it would continue to be European led and inspired. European deductive science would provide the answers to all puzzles regarding the universe, its properties and make up; the new social sciences would do the same in regard to humanity, while history would tell the tale of this advance of civilisation towards its culmination under European inspiration. It was not really questioned that part of the school's job was to inculcate these wise certainties into the minds of the young of Europe. For many national school systems, this mission was coupled with the task of teaching of the certainty of the divine Christian benevolence that kept watch over the relentless march of European technological, scientific, political, aesthetic and moral progress.

Of course, this Eurocentric perspective was matched by individual state ethnocentrism in the curricula of the schools of the various European states. Each state's curriculum, within a broad and seemingly non- problematic European framework, extolled the virtues of their own state, often exemplified through a roll call of the state's past great and good. Such a curriculum made and perhaps still makes a great deal of sense. It is patently obvious that the schools should teach all children the state language(s), the geography and economy of the state and its history. Equally, the science and maths curriculum should apparently teach knowledge appropriate to the needs of individuals who have to function economically within the state, rather than of those who have to survive sustainably within the ecosystem. But, as was argued in the last chapter, such bland curricular statements tell us little of what sort of knowledge should actually be taught in schools and universities. In the same manner, a European framework may be regarded as desirable only if it is clear what this means. In other words, it is important to know where Europe is, and who a European is, before the schools can teach anything sensible on this theme to children and young people. The problem here is that many of the answers that are given to such questions reflect older perspectives which are seldom questioned. In this chapter, these confusions are examined in some detail.

One starting point is the Greek poet Cavafy. In his poem 'Expecting the Barbarians' (Cavafy, 1961), the city fathers wait for the barbarians to arrive in order to surrender the keys of the city in the hope of ensuring their safety. Dressed in their best, they wait all day in the heat. No barbarians arrive which is not seen as a respite, because,

> Some people arrived from the frontiers,
> And they said that there are no longer any barbarians.

> And now what shall become of us without any barbarians?
> Those people were a kind of solution.
> (Cavafy, 1961 p.19)

So they go, fearfully, back into the city. Fearful, not just for their lives, but for what the non-appearance of the barbarians may signify. Equally worrying is when, on being encountered, the barbarians appear not to behave like barbarians. Hale quotes Valinano, a sixteenth century visitor to Japan:

> ...Valignano wrote that 'it may truly be said that Japan is a world the reverse of Europe; everything is so different and opposite that they are like us in practically nothing. So great is the difference in their food, clothing, honours, ceremonies, language, management of the household, in their way of negotiating, sitting, building, curing the wounded and sick, teaching and bringing up children, and in everything else, that it can be neither described or understood. Now all this would not be surprising', he continues in a telling passage, 'if they were like so many barbarians, but what astonishes me is that they behave as very prudent and refined people in all these matters. To see how everything is the reverse of Europe, despite the fact that their ceremonies and customs are so cultivated and founded on reason, causes no little surprise to anyone who understands such things (Hale, 1993, p.43).

An equally extreme statement of sixteenth century relativism can be found in Montaigne's essay, 'Of The Caniballes':

> I finde (as farre as I have beene informed) there is nothing in that nation, that is either barbarous or savage, unless men call that barbarisme which is not common to them. As indeed, we have no other ayme of truth and reason than the example and Idea of the opinions and customes of the countrie we live in (Montaigne, 1965, Volume I, p.219).

The sad thing is that the people of Europe, conventionally defined, continue to wait for the barbarians in fear and trepidation like Cavafy's city fathers. More, as we see the collapse of the former Yugoslavia and the consequent rise in religious and cultural hatreds that have accompanied it, it is necessary to ask why the educational systems, both there and elsewhere in Europe, have failed to counter effectively this continuing fear of the barbarians that lurks beneath the seemingly placid European surface. Yet to ask this question presupposes answers to the questions posed earlier in this chapter, namely, where and what is this Europe, who are these Europeans and indeed, who are the barbarians?

On the surface, these seem angels on the head of a pin type questions, the worst type of scholasticism. For, at the level of common sense, it is obvious where Europe is and who is a European. And although it might differ from state to state, within each state there would be some agreement as to who the barbarians are. However, as this chapter will attempt to demonstrate, the answers are not obvious, neither are they clear. It will be further argued that such a lack of clarity on these issues continues to help maintain a narrow eurocentricity in the states that currently make up the European Union and the education that they provide. That in turn helps bolster national ethnocentricity, xenophobia and racism, both in schools and universities and in the wider society that these institutions serve.

To help counter all of these, it is essential that schools and universities put forward a new perspective on definitions and histories of Europe and the European. Such definitions will continue to change as European demography, economics and politics continue to change and/or are redefined. In fact, the terms have always been conditional ones, changing their meaning as the various social contexts within which they are located have changed over time. In other words, to misquote Canning, we need better to understand the old Europe if we are to assert and make sense of the new, changing Europe.

4.2. 'The Extent of Their Dominions'

So, where is Europe? As a UK school atlas of the late 1830s put it:

> According to the decisions of modern science, Europe is bounded on the south by the Mediterranean sea, on the west by the Atlantic ocean, which includes the Azores Islands and Iceland; Greenland being considered a part of North America. On the north, its boundary is the Arctic ocean, comprehending the remote islands of Spitzbergen and Nova Zembla. Towards the east, the limits of Europe seem even yet to be inaccurately defined. Its natural and geographical boundaries might easily be obtained by tracing the river Ousa from its source to its junction with the Belaia, thence along the Kama to the Volga, which would constitute a striking natural division, to the town of Sarapta, whence a short line might be carried due west to the river Don, which would complete the unascertained line of demarcation. But this great outline, through the petty governments under the dominion of Russia, science has hitherto been prevented from adopting. (Russell, c.1838, p.iii.)

Much of the modern confusion is spelt out in this definition. It is seemingly scientific as well as 'natural', but politics clearly are important in relation to the most problematic border, namely that to the east. It also reveals the nineteenth century scientific perspective — a major element in the Enlightenment project — that everything could (and should) be accurately and objectively measured, catalogued and systematised.

In more modern times, the *Oxford Illustrated Dictionary* defines Europe as a 'Continent of N. hemisphere, western part of the land mass of the Old World, bordering on the Atlantic Ocean' (Coulson, 1980, p.288). The implication of this definition, like that of Russell some one hundred and fifty years earlier, is that the western part of the 'Old World' is roughly the same as the most widely accepted geographical definition of the *continent* of Europe, the boundary markers of which are the Urals, the Straits of Gibraltar and the Bosphorus. A more precise definition along these lines is that of the *Cambridge Encyclopaedia*, where Europe is defined as the 'Second smallest continent, forming an extensive peninsula of the Eurasian land-mass, occupying c. 8% of the Earth's surface, bounded N and NE by the Arctic Ocean, NW and W by the Atlantic Ocean, S by the Mediterranean Sea, and E by Asia beyond the Ural Mts.' (Crystal ,1990, p.423). Clear and precise as the definition appears, it is less scientific than its language implies. The water boundaries may seem reasonable, though where that leaves offshore islands like Britain, Corsica, Cyprus, Iceland and Ireland is unclear. Even less clear is the geographical privileging of a particular peninsula. It cannot be because of either its physical size or population, as India is larger on both counts.

The reason frequently put forward for this state of affairs is that Europe is a separate *continent*, along with the other six, namely, Africa, Antarctica, Asia, Australasia, North and South America. But the term continent is merely an operational division hallowed by long usage in schools and elsewhere. It is also important to note that the six were once four, viz. Europe, Africa, Asia and America (Russell, c. 1838) and before that, three. The poet John Donne (Donne, 1933, p.35) in the early 17th century described how

On a round ball
A workeman that hath copies by, can lay
An Europe, Afrique and an Asia,
And quickly make that, which was nothing, *All*.

Here, one is neither arguing for the abolition of a useful concept nor, necessarily, arguing against Europe, however defined, being a continent. The point is that Europe is a continent because the term originated from Europe at a time when it saw itself as the centre of the civilised world. There is little point in dividing up the world into geographically significant regions if your own region is omitted. Again, it is helpful to return to Russell at this point. His panegyric on Europe is as follows:

> This portion of the globe, though least in dimension, is of more importance than any other, not merely to its own inhabitants, but to all who think commerce, science and the arts, of any advantage to mankind. In modern times it has been the seat of literature; and its natives have been justly distinguished for their power, wisdom, courage and strength of intellect: of which, imperishable monuments may be found in the extent of their dominions, the purity of their religion, the principles of their legislation, and the comprehensiveness of their laws (Russell, c. 1838, p. iii).

This follows in a tradition which goes back at least to the Renaissance. Hale quotes Ortelius, who published an atlas in English in 1570, as saying of Europe that it 'is so pleasant and so beautiful with stately cities, townes and villages, that for the courage and valour of the people and several nations, although it be less in quantity and circuit, yet might it be accounted, and indeed of all the ancient writers hath it ever been accounted, superiour unto the other parts of the world' (Hale, 1993, p.14).

It is important to recognise that land boundaries of continents are a contentious and contested area, not just in Europe. For example, geographical textbooks and atlases have a problem with Central America. Some put it in the North American continent and some in the South American. Other textbooks and atlases get around the issue by calling one continent North and Central America, or Central and South America, in other words accepting there is an ambiguity and settling it on pragmatic or political grounds.

Other branches of science have similar difficulties. In ornithology, as Campbell and Lack (1985, p.147) assert, 'the continents of conventional geography do not provide a satisfactory framework in zoogeography'. Although national pride and pragmatic use may be gratified by national ornithological studies, the scientific study of birds, like those of other flora and fauna, has concentrated on larger, biologically homogenous areas, the zoogeographical regions (Cramp et al., 1977-1994). In this division of the world, conventional Europe becomes part of the Palaearctic, one of six major regions, roughly corresponding to the Eurasian tectonic plate. The boundaries of states have little purpose in such discussions. In short, science finds itself unable to accept the political definitions set up by the traditional European powers, definitions frequently enshrined within the curriculum of schools and universities throughout the European Union. However, as the Russell quote above indicated, science has not always been so dispassionate. It was not just a 'British disease' either. The nationalistic debates about the pre-eminence of German science in the eighteenth century shows how scientists can be swayed by xenophobia *within* their field (Schneider, 1989).

This discussion demonstrates that the commonplace, common sense definitions of Europe are neither objective nor scientific but are mainly political, socio-cultural and/or operational definitions, suiting particular ends. Consequently, it is not surprising that, as those ends have changed, so have the definitions. The concern is that people and states and education systems continue to make definitions on such grounds but do not accept and/or realise that they are doing so. As a result, such definitions are not seen for what they are but are regarded as scientific and objective facts, reinforced through long and seemingly uncontested usage.

Differing political definitions of Europe go back a great deal further than the last two hundred years. The first recorded mention of the concept is in the Homeric *Hymn to Apollo*, where it is defined as an area near the Hellespont, the reputed home of Europa. At that time, it was used to refer to the Greek mainland in contradistinction to the Greek islands of the Aegean. By the fifth century BC it was clear, in the Greek use of the term, that it was being used to distinguish the Greeks from people living in what is now called Asia (Encyclopaedia Britannica, 1947). Thus, from its origins, the term was used to define 'us' and 'our land' as opposed to the 'them' and 'their land'. In many ways, the term Europe continues to be used in this way. The problem is that it is no longer clear as to who the 'us' are and where is 'our land'.

In the succeeding centuries, people and nations within the area now referred to as Europe continued to define Europe in an exclusive and excluding way, although for much of this time the area under consideration was not described as Europe. For example, borders in the area were delineated as part of the process of the breaking up of the Roman Empire from the fourth century onwards. The boundaries of the Roman Empire changed rapidly during a period of human history when peoples were moving westwards across the Eurasian land mass. The break up of the Roman Empire into its Eastern and Western parts, and the successful consolidation of the Frankish Empire under Charlemagne was again, not a delineation of Europe. It was more a delineation of Latin and Greek Christendom, particularly exigent within the contemporary territorial and religious conflict with the new and expanding power of Islam.

Interestingly, a religious map of Christendom in the eleventh century would roughly correspond with the current dominant image of Europe, although where the Crusader Latin Kingdoms of the Middle East would fit in would be more problematic. The major difference was the Caliphate of Cordova in the Iberian peninsula, where Moslems, Jews and Christians created a multicultural society which the rest of Christendom feared and hated and whose memory has been almost forgotten in the collective European consciousness (Hale, 1993, pp.475-478). This position may differ in relation to the way this history is dealt with in Spanish textbooks, where efforts are being made to reevaluate that period of Spanish history. However, in the history books of many other European states it is generally treated, if at all, as an intrusion into the essentially homogenous flow of European (Christian) history.

By the fourteenth century, a map that showed the division between Christendom and Islam would have been even more like a map of the dominant contemporary vision of Europe. It was so for a brief period only, however. As the Ottoman Turks moved beyond the Bosphorus, their new and expanding empire soon included much of the Balkans. Indeed, by the time of the Treaty of Westphalia in 1648, the Ottoman Empire reached almost to Vienna. Moreover, the Turkish and Islamic presence in conventionally defined Europe has continued to the present day. Despite this historical and contemporary reality, much of the discourse about the concept of Europe within the states that now make up the European Union has continued to operate by excluding or ignoring this presence.

The boundaries of Europe have remained, and continue to remain obscure. For example, the views of the Russian biologist and Slavophile, Danilevsky, who, in the 1860s, argued for a clear division between an Orthodox Russian dominated Slavic Eurasia and a Latin Christian Europe were still influential in pre-1917 Russia. Indeed they may still indirectly influence the politics of the Balkans to this day (Balace, 1991; Delrot, 1992.) For example, the relations between Russia and Serbia (both Orthodox in historical terms) are different from the relations between Russia and the other states of the former Yugoslavia (Marr, 1993; Singleton, 1985).

Such views apart, perhaps the most significant area of difficulty was and, to a large extent remains, best exemplified by examining the position of the South Eastern border of Europe, a point touched upon earlier. This area has long been seen as a critical boundary, for example between Orthodox and Latin Christianity and between Christianity and Islam. It has moved backwards and forwards over time from the Balkans, via the Bosphorus to an indeterminate end in the Middle East. The keys to the positioning of this European boundary are 'race' and religion, the two often combining. And it is these two factors which continue to complicate the debate about both the positioning of Europe and the nature of the people who call themselves Europeans. The confusion is made worse by the continuation of the conflation of geographical position with moral and cultural worth. As an example of this, Hollister's classic American college primer *Medieval Europe*, published in 1964, shifts in one page from 'Europe' to 'Western Europe' to 'Western Civilisation' with hardly a seam showing.

One current and obvious example of this continuing confusion is the position of Turkey vis-a-vis the European Union. Is it, so some arguments go, really a *European* state? In other words, is this state really *in* Europe? Even when referred to as the 'sick man of Europe' in the nineteenth century, the main concern of other European powers was not so much with the sick man's health but with quarrelling over his soon-to-be relinquished possessions. It was as if, at last, the Turkish dominated part of Europe could be returned to its rightful 'owners'. This view has had a long history, added to and romanticised in the aftermath of Greek independence in 1832 (Bernal, 1987). One consequence of this misrepresentation in many of the dominant educational discourses within European Union states, is that the Turkish/Islamic presence within Europe is still implicitly regarded as invasive and 'non European'. The fact that Muslims, as well as Turks, have been part of conventionally defined Europe for hundreds of years is just not recognised. Sadly, it has taken the Bosnian civil war to make many people living in Europe aware of this historical diversity. Also, in how many education systems within the European Union are Turkish origin children described as coming from within Europe, as could legitimately be claimed?

Such a state of affairs makes it appear that Europe remains an excluding category masquerading as an objective spatial referent. We will, of course, continue to have to use it as a convenient label in everyday life, but should be more aware of the term's history. This is particularly true when Europe is used as a concept in contradistinction to another spatial referent, for example Asia, or when discussing which states should be part of the European Union, the Council of Europe or any other European-wide institution. A further part of this debate, again brought to the fore by discussions about Turkey, is whether this state's inhabitants are really 'Europeans'? For if their physical presence in Europe cannot be gainsaid, they can still be defined away, as it were, in cultural terms. To answer this latter question, the term 'European' needs to be examined.

4.3. 'Marked out by Nature'

The *Oxford English Dictionary* (Murray, 1933) does not define Europe but is comprehensive, and most interesting, in its definition of 'European'. Three related meanings are given: firstly, 'Belonging to Europe, or its inhabitants' (first used in 1603); secondly, 'Taking place in, or extending over, Europe' (first used in 1665); thirdly, 'A native of Europe' (first used in 1632). In the 1972 Supplement, (Burchfield, 1972) a further meaning is added, relating to the third one, interestingly enough also coming from the seventeenth century, this time from 1696. This fourth definition states that a European is a 'person of European extraction who lives outside Europe: *hence, a white person*, esp. in a country with a predominately non-white population' (emphasis added). By the time of the second edition (Simpson and Weiner, 1989), only the first two definitions had survived. A new third one had appeared, referring to new European institutions, first used in 1952. The ones that had disappeared seem to be the result of an anxiety about the past rather than a concern for lexicographical accuracy.

However, staying for a moment with all the older definitions, for the most part, from the time of the colonial expansion of the seventeenth century, the term European was, in English at any rate, synonymous with the white population of Europe, with even that problematic term (white), being taken as self evident. The interesting shift in perception that these definitions reveal is one from seeing a European as a person living in a Christian state, to that of a white person living in the same. In other words, not only has the shifting nature of the boundary been forgotten, but so has the fact that there has been a constant non-white presence in that area (Fryer, 1984; Shyllon, 1977).

These shifts of meaning, like those traced in relation to the defining of Europe, are not too surprising. The trouble, is that if a European is seen as a long fixed, rather than a constantly changing category, significant groups of the European population are excluded, being seen in some way, as non-European. It therefore should come as no surprise that the European-born descendants of more recent groups of migrants into Europe in the post war period are seen as some sort of non-European 'invasive' group of people by certain sections of the population. Because history books and lessons in schools and universities have not always taught how mixed the population of Europe has always been, there is the feeling that these particular groups of Europeans are 'foreigners'. It is perhaps legitimate for a state or superstate like the European Union to define its non-citizens as foreigners, but it is not logical nor legitimate to define citizenship through principles of exclusion that rest solely on perceptions of putative national identities. For how a state defines its citizenry is crucial. In other words, even before we define who exactly is a European we have to unravel the confusion as to who exactly is German, is French, is English and so on.

At an obvious level, a citizen is often considered a person born within the boundaries of a state. However, Europe's history, particularly its recent history, has been bedevilled by the confusion between a national *group* and a national *boundary*, the two rarely coinciding. One of the sadnesses of European history is that many politicians have claimed otherwise. Even so-called progressive politicians have played such chauvinistic cards. At the beginning of the French Revolution, Danton reiterated the view that France had 'natural boundaries' within which, presumably, French people lived or had the right to live. He claimed

The limits of France are marked out by nature. We shall reach them at their four points; at the Ocean, at the Rhine, at the Alps, at the Pyrenees (Quoted in Doyle, 1989, p.200).

Similar sentiments have, and still can be found expressed by politicians and others from within most European states. Russia and its 'near abroad' concern for ethnic Russians living outside its borders would be one contemporary manifestation. Concern about the large numbers of ethnic Germans spread across Europe has once again come upon the political agenda (Barber, 1994). Furthermore, two major European communal wars this century confirm the power of such 'natural' perceptions. Poor blameless 'nature' has a lot to answer for, though, as Milton said, 'Accuse not Nature, she hath done her part' (Milton, *Paradise Lost*, Book VIII, line 561).

The issue of how the citizens of European states perceive and define themselves is an important one and there is a commensurate literature (Breuilly, 1985; Edwards, 1985; Gellner, 1985). In the context of this chapter, it is argued that because of the absence of complementarity between the state and its contributing nationalities and ethnicities, many European states, through their institutions, and in particular through the provision of education, construct a fallacious ideal typical model of a European as well as of a state citizen. Both these models suggest that somehow Europe and Europeans belong to a small scale society somehow writ large. By this process the states of the European Union and their education systems attempt to disguise their fractured, paranoid and often predatory origins.

Such myths of national state unity and European identity are, in fact, partly a codification and legitimation of the dominant groups' social and economic arrangements and partly a reflection of dominant concepts of the nature of Europe and its citizens. As has been argued elsewhere (Jones, 1992) the model of the so-called nation state that has emerged through this process is not a nation in terms of the most common definitions, although the state may wish to assert that it is. The many nations, nationalities and/or groups contained within modern Europe and its constituent states are often ignored or submerged. At the state, or 'national' level this is done through the creation and propagation of state/'national' stereotypes and at the European level by a further set of stereotypes that ape the individual state/'national' ones. As Bhabha claims:

It is the mark of the ambivalence of the nation as a narrative strategy — and an apparatus of power — that it produces a continual slippage into analogous, even metonymic, categories, like the people, minorities or 'cultural difference' that continually overlap in the act of writing the nation (Bhabha, 1990, p.293).

Thus, many modern states claim that their citizens — the 'nation' — share some or all of the following: a common state language or languages; an agreed set of economic arrangements; a common state history ('heritage'), sometimes with agreed regional variations; a common religion, perhaps with denominational divisions, accepted, if not believed in, by all; finally, a common culture, often with a folk and elite variant.

In other words, a country is perceived as being a unified group, both a nation and a state. If there is internal opposition to this, which breaks out into conflict, it is called civil war. If the civil war brings about permanent division of the state, it becomes transmogrified by history into a liberation war. (This is not to deny the existence of real civil wars but is meant to indicate how the term can be abused.) In other words there is a constant tension between the nations that make up the modern state and the encompassing state itself, a tension that is seldom reflected in state-controlled curricula. Appadurai states this relationship well:

The relationship between states and nations is everywhere an embattled one It is possible to say that in many societies, the nation and the state have become one another's projects. That is, while nations (or more properly groups with ideas about nationhood) seek to capture or co-opt states and state power, states simultaneously seek to capture and monopolise ideas about nationhood (Appadurai, 1990, p.303).

This convergence of two different concepts is not new. It reflects a continuous debate about the nature of the nation and the nature of the state that has been conducted in Europe for at least the last three centuries (Delrot, 1992). Other definitions of a nation would include: a state's population, very much an Encyclopedist definition and one that inspired Danton; a group of people sharing common characteristics such as a language or a religion; a group of people who may or may not share common features such as language, but who perceive themselves and/or are perceived by others as being a nation; the citizenry of a state.

citizenry and in terms of legal rights and obligations, their powers are currently final, although being eroded in those states within the European Union. In terms of cultural rights and obligations, their remit is more limited and less clearly defined. This is no doubt part of the reason why so many states carefully control the curriculum of their schools. A pluralistic European identity on these late modern terms would contradict much in the existing curriculum within the schools and universities of the European Union and elsewhere in Europe.

That this redefining task is urgent is reinforced by the current low levels of understanding Europe that pertain, not just in schools, but also in universities throughout Europe. Peter Radcliffe, reporting on the UK test-site of a 1990 cross-European project on perceptions of Europe (Radcliffe, 1992), found that a significant minority of the sample of UK university students separated Britain from Europe while a majority saw Europe as consisting mainly of the European Union states. Radcliffe described this state of affairs as indicating 'the almost total invisibility of eastern and central Europe' (Radcliffe, 1992, p.35) and quotes a student as responding: 'I don't think of Eastern European countries as being truly 'European'; for me it's the countries from Germany westwards' (p.34).

Statements such as that support the view that the terms of concern of this chapter need urgent educational consideration. This chapter has so far attempted to demonstrate that the terms 'Europe' and 'European' are conventionally used in a rather similar way to the use of the term 'race' (Tierney, 1982). The position is put quite starkly by Sivanandan when he stated that 'we are moving from an ethnocentric racism to a Eurocentric racism, from the different racisms of the different member states to a common market racism' (Sivanandan, 1988, quoted in Radcliffe, 1992, p.30). In other words, it should be incumbent on people to explain not just *what* they mean by Europe and European but *why* they wish to use those classificatory terms. Although on the surface, they seem helpful, they should be examined constantly to see if their use is descriptive or political.

The consequences of such a perspective for the curriculum are marked, however, and are one of the principle concerns of this book. Just as ethnocentricity has to be combated and countered in the curriculum so must a false eurocentricity (see Chapter Nine). Much of the debate about a eurocentric curriculum argues for an international dimension to be laid against a European one. What has to be clarified are the boundaries of such a European curriculum, as well as its content. Again the political determinations of geography need to be made visible. In Science for example, the Ptolemaic cosmological system is often taught as a European contribution to scientific knowledge. Equally, his map of the world is often taught in Geography as one of the first European attempts to map the world. Yet Ptolemy was, by some of the definitions explored earlier in this paper, an African. Greek Alexandria in Egypt was one of the centres of scientific thought for nearly eight centuries. But where was Alexandria and who were the Alexandrines? Trying to claim it 'for us' (whoever 'us' are, or, indeed, 'them') seems a ridiculous act of educational xenophobia.

Such a state of affairs is, of course, not confined to Europe. It appears to be a feature of dominant groups of states elsewhere in the world. For example, the concept of Central America, it could be claimed, was brought into being to exclude Mexico from North America, in a remarkably similar way to the treatment of Turkey in the European context. Even new groupings, like the European Union and the North American Free Trade Area (NAFTA) do not really get over these exclusions. This definitional issue then, far from being an arid intellectual exercise, is crucial to our perception of a genuinely intercultural education for European states. If Europe's borders are recognised as being fluid, as indeed they are, and if a European becomes an including rather than an excluding category, as it should, then some essential first steps are taken in providing an appropriate political context within which a meaningful intercultural educational debate about Europe can take place.

Chapter Five

EUROPEAN CIVIC CULTURE: TRADITIONAL AND MODERNIST

5.1. Civic Culture and International Urbanisation

The last chapter focused on the social construction of Europe and Europeans and the consequence of this for education, particularly in respect of minorities. From this analysis, at least one key question follows and that is how the sense of *being* a European is put across in schools and universities across Europe. This chapter thus examines the notion of European civic culture and its relevance to school and university curricula. It further elaborates the classification of traditional, modernist and postmodern begun in Chapter Three. It also emphasises the role of educational institutions in the selection and reproduction of European civic culture from these forms of epistemological organisation. It is developed from an earlier formulation of civic culture (Coulby, 1992).

However, this concern with cultural selection within Europe should not be seen as an aspect of the ethnocentricity which has so often characterised that continent and which was examined in the previous chapter. Indeed, it is in the tensions and conflicts which surround notions of what it is to be a European citizen that the categories of this chapter operate. So it begins with a brief consideration of wider, global patterns of social and economic change and the ways in which they affect civic culture generally and European civic culture in particular. This stress on the civic, or urban aspect of culture is not derived entirely from our concerns with cities and with urban education (Bash et al, 1985; Coulby and Jones, 1992). Parts of Europe like Germany, the Netherlands and England are amongst the most urbanised areas in the world. It is in their cities (and many other European cities as

The European Union is not the only international political organisation, though it is currently backed by considerable economic force and political momentum. The former Soviet Union has disappeared into a fracture of national states during the same period in which many people in Europe have aspired to solidify the European Union into an enlarged and unitary state. For the purposes of this chapter however, it is necessary to note only the fragility of the units of analysis. In order to understand the social and educational issues and policies in many European cities it is increasingly necessary to shift the unit of analysis continually from the city to the state to the European Union and to the rest of the world.

Moreover, in returning to the examination of cities, what common language is there, to talk about such differing cities and the educational issues and conflicts that arise in them? How can their contrasts be expressed without lapsing into the discredited polarities of first and third world, or the patronising and misleading vocabulary of developing or emergent nations? Even to speak of levels of urbanisation or industrialisation implies a continuum or a historical process through which all cities travel before arriving at the state of alleged perfection currently exemplified by certain Western European or North American urban areas. Apart from the ethnocentricity of such classifications, they embody assumptions about economic growth within a world system fractured by financial and military exploitations.

This exploitation is becoming more rather than less exacerbated. Whilst in 1960 the richest fifth of the world's population earned 30 times the income of the poorest fifth; today it earns 60 times more' (Brazier, 1994, p. 6). If terms extrinsic to the city are chosen as social indicators or categories then the difficulties encountered with regard to the geographical unit of analysis are solidified. The differences between cities are then codified in terms drawn from the state, political and economic organisation, cultural heritage, gross national product, per capita income and so on. Whilst, as indicated above, the oscillation between the various geographical units of analysis can be managed, a post-modern analysis would demand that it always be sensitive to non-typical, non-conformist or openly dissident urban areas.

It is in terms of the differences *within* cities that there may well be common urban and urban educational themes: even between such apparently differing cities as, say, Pittsburgh (Thomas and Moran, 1992) and Nairobi (Lillis, 1992). These, like other cities, are the geographical focus of more widespread social and economic differences between groups. The extremes of wealth and poverty are present in both Nairobi and Pittsburgh. Certainly there is a relativity: the extremely poor are much poorer in Nairobi and there are many more of them as a percentage of the population of the city. In each case, however, the city concentrates and makes highly visible, the contrasts between the rich and the poor.

This concentration and visibility means that conflict over scarce resources, not least education, between the rich and poor are more likely, more extreme and, in turn, more visible in urban areas. Financial wealth, is not, of course the only difference between groups within urban areas and in earlier writing (for instance Coulby and Jones, 1989) examples were offered of the various ways in which urban diversity could be categorised. However, one of the major reasons that it is valuable to conduct international urban and urban educational studies is that large urban areas across the globe are sites of such highly visible differences and of conflicts between different groups (Harvey, 1981).

The other major reason to justify the study of urban educational issues is that the pattern of global urbanisation makes it impossible to separate developments in one city from financial, political and military events elsewhere. The international division of labour (Frobel et al., 1988) has speeded up not only investment and disinvestment decisions but also movements of people within and between states looking for work and wealth in the areas favoured by high investment or strong commodity prices. Neither the new international division of labour nor the pattern of urbanisation that has accompanied it are fixed conditions. The international division of labour changes with increasing rapidity according to capital flows, market penetration and the consolidation of economic weight into political pressure. Examples of this would include the emergence and expansion of the European Union and the states of the Pacific rim, as well the military adventures of the USA. The resultant changes in urbanisation, urban economic activity and urban form are as tangible in Strasbourg as in Seoul.

Moreover, both the number of large cities and their actual size continues to grow, in China and Turkey as well as in South Asia, Africa and Latin

America. European urban pride has to recognise that the ten largest (10 million people plus) cities are *not* in Europe (*Times Atlas of the World*, 1991, p.44). Yet such urban growth runs alongside events in the Middle East, the former Soviet Union and Eastern Europe that have revealed the fragility of states despite their appearance of solidity and permanence. The international pattern of increasingly interactive and still expanding cities remains a key economic and political phenomenon, one that is perhaps more important than similar processes between the states within which they are located. Despite wide variations in both the contexts and the levels of social provision in these cities, no single urban area can be understood in isolation. The developing international division of labour, capital and decision-making means that the economic, political and, increasingly, educational development of cities in widely separated states are inextricably interlinked.

5.2. Semiology and the city

This international interdependence and commonality of urban systems is not always reflected in the ways in which cities are portrayed and understood. This gap between the image of the city and people's day to day experience of it is one which is manifested in the curricula of many urban schools in Europe, as elsewhere. It is necessary to understand the semiology of the city as one of the dislocations between the international political, economic, cultural and demographic influences which characterise all urban systems and the romantic, nationalist influences which inform so many of their school curricula. The planning and architecture of different cities are not merely a matter of appearance: 'Society ... is to a large extent constituted as well as represented through the buildings and spaces that it creates' (King, 1990c, p.404).

Furthermore, the appearance of real and imagined cities appeals not only to the imagination but to the perceived forms of society, and has done so for centuries in Europe. For example, Kostof (1993), in discussing urban form, quotes Giovanni Botero's sixteenth century definition of a city as 'a congregation of people drawn together to the end they may thereby the better live at their ease in wealth and plenty'. Such optimism about urban life has always to be set against the more gloomy comments on cities made by many other writers. In other words, the city sits Janus-like at the centre of European social life. Its spaces and landscapes are the necessary arenas for the political, economic and social actions which themselves serve to reproduce and adjust such architectural and planning forms.

To focus on the signing or semiotics of cities is in no way to escape into a vague culturalist approach. Zukin's concept of landscapes helps further to identify the ways in which the visible form of cities and the ways in which they economically and politically function are interrelated:

> In a narrow sense, *landscape* represents the architecture of social class, gender and race relations imposed by powerful institutions. In a broader sense, however, it connotes the entire panorama that we see: both the landscape of the powerful — cathedrals, factories and skyscrapers — and the subordinate, resistant or expressive vernacular of the powerless — village chapels, shantytowns, and tenements. A landscape mediates, both symbolically and materially , between the socio-spatial differentiation of capital implied by *market* and the socio- spatial homogeneity of labour suggested by *place* (Zukin, 1991, p. 16).

The rural-urban dichotomy/continuum still has power in the European Union and North America but more at the level of symbol than of social experience. The escapist version of a rural arcadia is still held by many urban dwellers in England as a contrast to the alienation of their own lives. Indeed, in the UK the Prince of Wales has developed on his own estates what can only be called modern rural village housing estates, in a conscious and deliberate attempt to bring the convenience of the urban and the nostalgia of the rural into happy combination. Such artificial creations, like the Ebeneezer Howard-inspired garden suburbs of the early twentieth century, or similar experiments in New Delhi or Casablanca are an exercise in the literal building of myth, for if they work and people continue to live in them, they become urbanised and urban. Fred Inglis summed this up nostalgically, when he made the connection to education in these terms:

> The great myth survives in a larger pattern: the Garden Cities, and their descendants, the New Towns; the Town and Country Planning Acts; the National Parks; above all, the best of England's new schools, the homely, wholesome variety of the one-story English primary school in its own ground; all these speak eloquently of the gentle liberal herbivore and his small successes in the path of the industrial man-eaters (Inglis, 1973, p.12).

The urban English primary school maintains its frog pond and nature garden with dogged determination and the 'liberal herbivores' continue to do what they have always done, allowing themselves to be put out to grass. Arcadian bliss is, however, primarily a myth of elites living in long-established urban societies such as T'ao Yuan Ming in T'ang China, Virgil in Imperial Rome and Henry Thoreau in the rapidly industrialising nineteenth century United States. Today, as in former times, in Europe as in many other parts of the world, widespread rural poverty continues to make urban living seem attractive. The continuing migration to large cities is the dramatic evidence of this. For some the city is a sign of the possibility of economic prosperity and political and cultural freedom, for many others the symbol of exploitation and alienation.

The importance of the semiology of the city is increasingly recognised in urban studies (Harvey, 1989; King, 1990a; 1990b; Zukin, S. 1988; 1991). European cities, like those in the United States, embody an eschatology in their mean streets and high living. The city as heaven and hell is a potent image within urban literature and film. The examples are so numerous that any selection must be idiosyncratic: Chandler, Dickens, Grass, Rushdie, Simenon, Zola, Ellroy; *Alphaville, La Dolce Vita, Bladerunner, Metropolis, Manhattan, The Third Man, The Good Fellas, Raging Bull.* The eschatology is between the city as locale of (and sign for) violence and intolerance and the city on a hill dispensing political, moral and cultural certainties to the benighted lowlands. Crime fiction provides the most striking and violent presentations of the diabolic aspect of this imagery but it can be detected in many other genres and forms as well as in the metaphors of politicians and press. The idealised city is less common, residing most frequently in mythology, fantasy or idealism, Camelot, Minas Tirith, Utopia. The idealised city has only been essayed as part of the imperialist or post-imperialist dream in cities like New Delhi, Casablanca or Brasilia (Rabinow, 1989).

Although the contrast between city and rural village has little power as an analytic tool within the highly urbanised European Union countries, in many states, especially France, Germany and the UK, an idealised version of rural living is perceived as a retreat from the many hardships of urban life. The old (and misunderstood) Tonnies' dichotomies are revived within the strident signifiers of advertising, soap operas, clothing fashions or the leisure industry. Indeed, some sociological writing at times reads like the advertisers' copy. Sorokin and Zimmerman's classic 1929 study of the contrasts between urban and rural life extols rural life in the following supposedly objective sociological terms:

> Can... a city environment and manner of living satisfy these fundamental impulses and habits developed in quite a different situation and adapted to quite a different environment? The answer is no. Neither the impulses for creative activity, nor for orientation, curiosity, and novelty; nor the lust for variety and adventure; nor the physiological necessity for being in touch with nature; nor to enjoy with eyes the greenishness of the meadow; the beauties of the forest; the clear rivers; the waves of golden wheat in the field; nor to hear the birds singing; the thunderstorm, or the mysterious calm of an evening amidst nature; these and thousands of similar phenomena have been taken from the urban man (Sorokin and Zimmerman, p.466).

Whilst urban sociologists (such as Lee and Newby, 1983) may see this and other related urban-rural dichotomies or continua as discredited notions, they retain power at the romantic and imaginative level for all those who look forward to escaping from the city at weekends, on holidays or at some point in the future, to a rural world of cottages, nature and auberges. However, a less superficial way of understanding the conflicts over culture, knowledge and value which is taking place within cities, not least those of the European Union, might be in terms of three competing versions of European civic culture.

5.3. Traditionalist European Civic Culture

This book suggests that there are three versions of European civic culture, or more widely (in Chapters Seven and Nine) of knowledge systems: the traditional, the modern and the postmodern (the latter more a development of the modern than a version *sui generis*). All three versions of civic culture are ways of seeing the history, society, technology and artistic activity of the continent. However, the terminology may need clarification because of the level of generality. It is not being suggested that European culture is exclusively the product of European cities and towns, nor that there are only three forms of this culture. Culture is the complex product of different groups of people operating in groups as small as the family or as large as a prominent religious group or social class. It consists not only of products but also of rituals and practices. Child-rearing, the preparation, presentation and consumption of food and drink sit uneasily alongside the diverse literary, artistic, religious, musical and constructive products in any uneasy attempt to make generalisations about culture (see, for example, Williams, 1981). Given the multitude of cultures across Europe, it is obviously a crude simplification to categorise all this activity within three main headings or even to conceptualise European civic culture as an identifiable phenomenon at all. The purpose of offering categories at this level of generalisation is to establish some conception of diverse and shifting social phenomena and their subsequent representation in school curricula. The test for this typology is not as intellectual abstractions but as terms which have real purchase on social, especially educational, policy.

This chapter thus distinguishes between traditional, modernist and postmodern forms of European civic culture. This preliminary distinction allows for a contrast which firmly isolates and characterises traditional civic culture before the more elaborate classification of knowledge systems is made in Chapters Seven and Nine. It needs to be stressed that the categorisation of traditional, modernist and postmodern European civic cultures is not an attempt to offer a comprehensive classification of curricular systems. It is rather that this classification is a helpful one in isolating important aspects of (especially traditionalist) curriculum definition. One important new aspect is the extent to which an emergent European urban triumphalism is in danger of replacing state nationalisms as a limiting force in curricula.

Defining European civic culture is increasingly a political activity. Following on from the argument put forward in Chapter Four, it should be seen as part of that process through which states attempt to identify themselves with nations. It is a process which Sharma's study of the formation of Dutch identity clearly delineates as taking shape through a wide range of cultural manifestations (Sharma, 1991). In this process, as Smith discusses, education is a crucial instrument:

> They must be taught who they are, where they came from and whither they are going. They must be turned into co-nationals through a process of mobilisation into the vernacular culture, albeit one adapted to modern social and political conditions. ... Old religious sages and saints

can now be turned into national heroes, ancient chronicles and epics become examples of the creative national genius, while great ages of achievement in the community's past are presented as the nation's 'golden age' of pristine purity and nobility. The former culture of a community which had no other end beyond itself, now becomes the talisman and legitimation for all manner of 'national' policies and purposes, from agricultural villagisation to militarism and aggrandisement (Smith, 1990, p.184).

If the full diversity of cultural achievement in European cities is to be recognised then both the dominant traditional and modern notions must be challenged. Traditional European civic culture has achieved dominant status not only through state and civic endorsement and subsidy of concert halls and art exhibitions; it is also achieved through national curriculum programmes and through the control of research agenda in higher education. However, it is within educational institutions that the modernist programme has most successfully challenged traditional European civic culture. (On the transition from traditional to modern within education systems, see Archer, 1984.) Traditional civic culture is maintained by the increasingly close, but variable relationships between states, relationships between national and civic government, traditional artistic activity, mass media, religious institutions and education systems.

What this chapter terms traditional European civic culture celebrates the 'civilisation', itself a vexed term, its protagonists see as having been established on that part of the globe and, effectively, nowhere else. They would point to the achievements of specific European cities as the unquestionable history of the whole of human civilisation. Specific European cities are seen as the physical embodiment and repository not only of European history but of human achievement: Athens, Rome, Florence, Paris, Amsterdam and London.

Such a civilisation or culture will be seen in terms of particular activities and outstanding proponents (almost all of them men). Literature, for example, is seen as an agreed canon of classic texts from Aeschylus to Yeats. The art canon is perhaps more complex (Williams, 1994), but the traditionalist view would very likely include Greek architecture and sculpture as well as the 'great' names such as Leonardo, Michelangelo, Rembrandt, Turner, Manet, Cezanne and Picasso. Similarly, 'classical' music is seen to be largely the product of the German- and Italian-speaking states. Within this European civic culture, scientific and technological activities are present but less valued: Galileo's fate is still remembered.

Certain religious beliefs and practices can be seen as traditional and anti-modern, as exemplified by official Catholic statements on birth control or wider Christian concern over Sunday trading and women priests. It is not only in Ireland that modernist civic culture has failed to displace these values, though politics as well as family patterns and education in that country may provide rich examples. Although demographic data (Noin and Woods, 1993) indicate that the size of families no longer reflects conformity with the teaching of the Catholic Church, even in the countries of the South of Europe, and economic forces are gradually establishing seven days of consumerism across the European Union, there is no doubt that traditionalist religious beliefs and practices maintain a strong presence in traditional civic culture. This can clearly be seen in certain schools and higher educational institutions throughout Europe, where such religious views still predominate. However, the growth of liberation theology indicates that not all religious involvement in education is to be categorised as traditional rather than modernist.

The traditionalism of certain migrant groups in Europe, again often connected with religious beliefs and practices, can also lead to conflict with modernist school systems or with the traditionalist civic cultures still covertly espoused within them. These conflicts can be over food and clothing as well as compulsory denominational religious education and acts of worship. In France, as was briefly discussed in Chapter Three, conflicts over Islamic girls wearing traditional costume have taken a particularly ironic form. Islamic girls have been excluded from school for not conforming to the secularist norms so important to the Republic (Nundy, 1994). Ostensibly the modernist, post-revolutionary state is refusing to tolerate traditional civic culture. However, since this occurs at a time when the Republic is failing to reverse the expansion of denominational schooling, it may be that it is actually a clash between Catholic and Islamic culture which is being played out within the rhetoric of modernist secularism (Kepel, 1993). Or, just as likely, it is a manifestation of racism. Even more confusingly, it may be also symptomatic of a modernist state failing to deal with a late modern citizenry. A similar analysis could be made regarding the repeated denial of funding by the UK government to Islamic groups seeking to gain voluntary aided (VA) or voluntary controlled status for their schools. This refusal sits uneasily beside state funding of Protestant, Catholic and Jewish schools and higher education institutions:

> If you want to deny us VA schools, you must deny them to everybody. Let's not have them. I'd be 100 per cent with that. But at present the position is very clear. The right exists (Khan-Cheema, quoted in Pyke, 1994, p.12).

In practice, Islamic schools in the UK have successfully developed independently of state funding. The resulting institutions have been described as demonstrating a polarity:

> a school for Muslims or a Muslim school. ... Within the former, the institution offers a quasi-British education with aspects of Islam and Islamic studies grafted on where appropriate and subject to funding. The latter model, however, aims to provide a totally Islamic ethos within an Islamic framework, incorporating the Islamisation of knowledge and staffed solely by Muslim teachers able actively to impart the faith (Parker-Jenkins, 1994, p.13).

Whilst the former might be seen as an attempt to assert the traditional within the modern, the latter uses the context of postmodernism to provide the opportunity for a vigorous re-assertion of traditional values and knowledge.

Traditionalist civic culture in education is not restricted to the influence of religious beliefs and institutions. Movements in Denmark and England, for example, to try to establish some connection between the school and its perceived community may also be seen as manifestations of traditionalism (Carlsen, and Borga, 1993). The community with which educationalists are attempting to relate is seen to be unitary, organic and somehow healthy and positive. The community school movement may be seen as an attempt to dissociate education from the heterogeneity of urbanised Europe and from the pressures of modernism. The curriculum, for young children especially, may reflect a similar trend, valuing folk art, folk dancing and folk music against the technological products and activities of modernist civic culture. In Germany and Scotland, for example, both educational and civic institutions have long successfully sought to retain and enhance these aspects of culture (Harvie, 1994).

However, the argument over community education's traditionalist roots has to be set against some postmodernist commentators' concern for imagined communities. Bauman's powerful argument that 'community is now expected to bring the succour previously sought in the pronouncements of universal reason and their earthly translations: the legislative acts of the national state' (Bauman, 1992, p.xix), points to the links between certain exponents of postmodernity and traditionalist elements in society.

5.4. European Civic Culture and the Curriculum

It is particularly in curricular terms that education systems in Europe must make decisions about which view of European civic culture a particular state chooses to advocate and reproduce. As states revise their curricular and assessment systems they take decisions about which version(s) of European civic culture will affect the future.

Education systems must determine whether they are aiming to develop all their pupils and students or merely those representing particular social, cultural or linguistic groups. They must also, of course. determine the manner in which they wish boys and girls to be educated. They need to decide what arrangements would allow educational institutions to prepare young people for the unpredictable European and international workplace of today and the future, instead of the illusory but seemingly secure nationalistic certainties of yesterday. Such preparation is, of course, a major determinant of curricular policy and design across Europe. And, as in other parts of the book, certain critical curriculum areas, such as language, history and religion, keep demanding attention for the way in which they reproduce key elements of the traditional, modern and postmodern debate. In this chapter, with its focus on civic culture, the three that are considered are the curricular choices that have to be made in languages, literature and history.

It is self-evident that decisions must be made about languages. From the point of view of traditional European civic culture the favoured languages will be Latin and Classical Greek, the languages of traditional greatness. Another attractive language would be French, the language of civilisation, culture and eighteenth century diplomacy, although the teaching of French might be seen as being commensurate with the triumph of modernism. However, French is increasingly being replaced by the teaching of English, the language of the United States and scientific, imperialistic and commercial modernism.

However, it is more probably the extent to which European states' education systems acknowledge their regional linguistic diversity as well as the urban linguistic diversity resulting from demographic change that may be why postmodernist versions of European civic culture are becoming current. In respect of language this is by no means large (see Chapter Nine). At the time of writing, the break up of the former Yugoslavia offers revealing debates about the status and position of languages within a state. Before the collapse, the dominant language of Yugoslavia was Serbo-Croat. Now, the name carries a historical legacy that many of its speakers would wish to deny. Serbian, Bosnian, Croatian are all now spoken; sometimes the issue is avoided by simply calling the language used 'my language', that is, it needs no label for it is mine and my people's.

From language debates to debates about the teaching of literature written in those languages is but a short step. The canons of literature to be studied are easy to determine within the values of traditional European civic culture. As discussed earlier, in Chapter Three, they would contain a list of the 'great and the good' from Europe, rubbing shoulders with a similar group writing in the language of instruction. Most would be safely dead, white and male.

Other curricula areas would share similar orientations. Traditional fine arts and philosophy also, retaining a high prominence in the curriculum right up to higher education level, would similarly reflect such sexist and elitist priorities. These links between traditionalist curricula, xenophobia, militant nationalism and sexism are tellingly explored in the collection of essays examining textbooks in the former Yugoslavia (Rosandic and Pesic, 1994). Not surprisingly, literature and history are the key areas. The analysis is all the more forceful as it was written while the war in former Yugoslavia was in progress.

> This text was chosen because the *bones* and *graves* of those killed in action have a constitutive meaning for the people's suffering, its *greatness, power and glory* determines its right to a state and specific territory (even today it is often said that graves and bones define Serbia's borders) (Pesic, 1994, p 73).

As suggested earlier in this chapter, modernist civic culture would place a lower priority on literature, fine arts and philosophy and more emphasis on science and mathematics. However, modernism's contribution civic culture has frequently been to give them a further nationalistic and xenophobic emphasis (see Chapter Six). From the perspective of postmodernist civic culture, it would be necessary to question the whole notion of an accepted and orthodox canon and to ensure that pupils and students were exposed to a wide variety of material from across Europe and beyond and appropriate priority placed on the cultural products and activities of the whole range of European urban groups. This is not merely to establish an alternative canon but to bring into the view of pupils and students the processes and criteria by which canons come to be established.

Traditionalist versions of history stress national heritage, and frequently extol it. As Shennon notes

> A recent CDCC report confirms that 'the French were overwhelmingly convinced of the significance of their revolution for the world, of the superiority of their revolution compared with the American and Russian ones' (Shennan, 1991, pp 44-45).

Again the former-Yugoslavian textbooks provide an extreme, but by no means untypical example:

> One example will suffice: the text book for the 7th grade says that in World War I Serbia suffered a toll of 1,200,000. 'But, the author says, 'its prestige mounted'. The figure is frightening, and so is the attitude towards it. One million victims helped the fatherland to win prestige. In other words, the sacrifice served its purpose. Nothing is said about the social, economic, civilisational and biological consequences of a loss of one quarter of the population. Nothing is said about this even in other, more relevant places which means that it is a general attitude to death and loss. ... The attitude towards the UN sanctions is a good example of the result such awareness produces. The political propaganda did not shape it; it merely instrumentalised it. ...Brimming with xenophobia, contempt and hatred for neighbouring nations, European and the world community, such texts fit well into the propaganda system which has made this war psychologically possible (Stojanovic, 1994, pp. 102-109).

The National Curriculum for History in England and Wales has already been cited as another example of a traditionalist, nationalistic curriculum. Further examples can be derived from a recent report on a symposium on the history curriculum and nationalism:

> Marie Homerova, a teacher at a Czech secondary school ... did admit ... that already since the division of Czechoslovakia into the Czech Republic and Slovakia, textbooks had appeared which treated the other as the 'enemy'. ... Mariusz Misztal, director of the English Language College, Pedagogical University of Cracow said 'In my opinion it will be impossible for east European countries to give up a nationalistic perspective. It has been said that nationalism is bad — and that can be true. But it is also important to have the feeling of belonging to a group, and history teachers in Poland will not be persuaded that it is better to do social history or world history' (Rafferty, 1994, p. 18).

Modernist versions of history emphasise progress and *The Triumph of the West* (the title of the BBC's televised version of Roberts, 1980). A further modernist possibility is that as individual state ethnocentric versions of history are gradually eroded they will be replaced by a European triumphal version of world history and current events. However, in England and Wales, where a National Curriculum in History is established by statute, as in many cases in the emergent curricula of eastern Europe, there is currently little evidence of such a shift from ethnocentrism to Eurocentrism.

Again using the National Curriculum in England and Wales as an example, it is possible to spell several ways in which modernist knowledge is in conflict with any education appropriate to the multicultural population and international aims of the UK. Firstly, as a nationalist curriculum, it is in conflict with large sections of the population of the state. As has been argued previously:

> If the compulsory and state-endorsed curriculum finds no room for various groups' literary products, ignores or travesties the part they have played in the history of the world, of Europe and of the UK, relegates their languages to the second division where they need never be a matter of any interest to any white child, and subject their children to the practices of an alien religion, then these groups will experience schools as increasingly hostile places. If those white pupils and parents who are racist are allowed to celebrate English triumphalist history or literature or to use the terms of the (1988) Act itself to minimise the cultural acknowledgement of other groups in the daily life of the school, then educational institutions are playing a part in raising and

75

exacerbating racial and group conflicts instead of reducing and resolving them (Coulby, 1991, p.37).

Secondly, this nationalist curriculum is at variance with the UK's membership of the European Union and with that process of Europeanising school knowledge to which member states are ostensibly committed (though see Chapter Nine for the limitations of this initiative). Indeed this curriculum might be seen to reflect and seek to reproduce that Europhobia which lies behind the current government's policy with regard to the implementation of the Maastricht Treaty. Finally, the nationalist curriculum undermines the UK's aspiration to remain a significant force in world trade and a major player in international politics.

> By limiting the nation's language skills to those of the EC and by not maximising the advantages which could be derived from its multilingual population, and by the encouragement of ethnocentrism and insularity, the National Curriculum fails to encourage the attitudes and skills needed successfully to develop the UK's economic and political role beyond the EC (Coulby, 1991, p.37).

Postmodern civic culture would stress that pupils and students in the European Union need to understand not only the history that is gradually bringing them together as Europeans, but also the history that attempts to place Europe in a non-dominant interpretation of the world. This should not just be a litany of guilt about imperialism, slavery and genocide — though it is hard to see how these topics can be avoided — it can include a recognition of achievements outside Europe and the ways in which these have or have not impinged on European development. (For a preliminary attempt to internationalise the European curriculum at secondary level see Shennan, 1991.)

To categorise traditionalist, modernist and postmodern European civic cultures leaves many questions unanswered. These refer, in particular, to how traditional modernist or postmodern alternatives are determined and implemented in the educational policy of states and of the European Union as a whole. If the categorisation points to crucial differences in how European curricular systems may be understood, then a whole range of questions arise, about the people, groups and institutions in individual states whereby particular views of European civic culture are determined, challenged or reproduced in education systems. These matters are considered in Chapter Seven. For the European Union itself, the Treaty of Maastricht opens vast possibilities for the development of European education. Some of these curricular possibilities are explored later, in Chapter Nine.

What remains to be investigated is how far this categorisation of civic culture is helpful in understanding the systems of behaviour and belief in cities outside Europe. Such a categorisation may be less helpful in understanding school and higher education curricula in other regions. Moving towards a fuller understanding of the civic culture of cities in other regions is therefore obviously an important task for the proponents of postmodern civic culture.

Finally, concepts of varieties of civic cultures need a finer examination if their full potential is to be exploited. The cities of Europe are remarkable for their demographic and cultural diversity. Indeed, it is this very diversity that partly forms the basis for the claim that a postmodern or late modern civic culture is emerging in the cities of Europe and that the tensions that arise from this are replicated in education systems. A key element in this cultural complexity is how states and groups within states define themselves and others and relate this differentiation to educational provision. These issues are the concern of the next chapter.

Chapter Six

DIFFERENTIATION
AND MODERNITY

6.1. Human Rights and the Political Definition of Minorities

The assumption is made frequently that the modern educational agenda is axiomatically accepted across Europe by state education systems. Central to this assumption is that the state's citizens, and by implication their children, have certain rights, expectations, duties and obligations. These may also be enshrined in the individual state's laws and educational practices and indeed, frequently are. They are seen as key characteristics of a modern state. Laws, statements of intent and declarations by states and their educational systems are, however, mainly normative statements. For many disadvantaged groups in Europe, the key educational issue is whether educational *practice* actually realises those legal rights, expectations, duties and obligations, and provides a full, effective and fulfilling education for their young people.

Normative statements and disadvantaged groups' educational aspirations do, however, suggest that a ready answer can be given to two anterior questions, namely, how are the various groups that make up a state defined in relation to education in the first place and, why should such groups have special educational rights, whether disadvantaged or not? These questions are complex, given that broad statements of educational rights should cover the aspirations of all citizens. On the other hand, if one of the purposes of a state's educational system is to inculcate a sense of national unity and national identity, it is likely that such an aim may well be in conflict with the educational (and other) aspirations of some of these groups.

Traditionally, discussions on such educational rights are similar to those on the aims of education, viz the potential for conflict between individual and group aspirations and between these and the needs of the state to have the education system provide a skilled, united and law-abiding citizenry. And here, in a variety of rhetorics, many states, in Europe and elsewhere, are quite explicit in stating that the primary objective of their educational system is the promotion of national unity and/or economic development. Those that are not explicit generally see it as self evident. The encyclopaedic three-volume *International Handbook of Educational Systems* (Cameron et al.,1984) confirms this, detailing the narrow range of educational objectives that states adopt. Amidst the concern for economic growth and social well-being, statements reflecting concerns for the proper education of minorities can be found, but rarely to the forefront of government thinking in relation to education. Even where specific reference is made to their educational rights, it is still the common practice that it is the state which defines who are the minorities, who are the disadvantaged, and what educational rights and especial provision they should have. Seldom do the groups concerned have a powerful voice in these processes, particularly if they are politically or economically weak.

The picture should not be seen as all gloom however. One of the achievements of the Enlightenment project has been its concern for the clarification of individual and state rights and responsibilities in relation to the dispossessed and disadvantaged. A series of key documents have been produced, starting with the United States Declaration of Independence (1776), the Virginia Bill of Rights (1776) the first ten amendments (enacted 1791) to the US Constitution and the French Declaration of Rights of 1789. Many of the aspirations of these documents can be found in contemporary international declarations such as those produced under the auspices of the United Nations and the Council of Europe. However, it is important to note here that despite their secular orientation for the most part, the various documents reflect Western Christian influenced values, in particular the prioritising of the individual's rights against those of the collective. In addition, it is also worth mentioning that the earlier documents left many issues either unseen or unresolved. Examples of the former would be rights relating to children and of the latter, rights relating to slaves.

In relation to education, the rights of children and young people are clearly important, although such concern must be placed within an appreciation of the specific social construction of childhood that dominates much European thought and which has played such a significant part in the modern agenda. The 1989 UN Convention on the Rights of the Child appears to provide the cap-stone to this part of the agenda, being an internationally agreed set of principles that give children, not just the right to survival but also rights to protection and to personal development free from discrimination. Despite its obvious and laudable intentions, the Convention marks the domination of the European Rousseauesque paradigm of childhood and implies the inferiority of other definitions and subsequent practices. This caveat aside, the declaration's general acceptance indicates that most states formally approve of the centrality of a modernist perspective that espouses rights, including educational rights, for all children.

At this point it is important to emphasise that most European states *do* recognise many of the minorities residing within their territory and accept that there are other groups, such as the poor and the disabled who are frequently also disadvantaged. The real issues for European education systems are whether the state acknowledges a specific minority or group or does not, whether the recognition of some group's or minority's existence by the state gives rise to appropriate educational practices and finally, whether these have the approval of the groups or minorities concerned. Stating a concern for such issues in relation to education, an important tenet in the modern agenda, does not ensure that such educational practices and rights actually exist. Such matters will be discussed in more detail later in this chapter.

It is, then, an important task to examine the definition of such groups and, in particular, the definition of educational minorities. It is also important to be clear as to who controls and legitimates the actual definition of such groups of people. To take the first task, that of minority definition, it is, at one level, a term that is in contradistinction to the term majority. But that distinction also raises problems. If the majority/minority distinction is being made in terms of numbers, then, as was mentioned earlier, the poor and women, although frequently discriminated against in their daily lives, are not minorities. If in terms of access to economic, political and educational power, some minorities, such as the rich, are very powerful. Sometimes, other types of minorities can be powerful in other ways, although such power is often perceived contentiously. A stigmatised minority, denied access to traditional routes to social mobility, may concentrate on those areas of social life where the barriers are lower, frequently using education as the ladder to surmount the barrier. A classic historical example would be the way in which Jewish people in the states of Europe, denied social mobility during the nineteenth and (most of) the twentieth centuries, concentrated on those areas in which they were allowed some measure of freedom and control, such as education. One consequence was their prominent position in the intellectual life of that period.

The second question, namely the nature of the defining process, lies at the heart of one of the key debates in postmodernity, namely the construction and representation of identities. If dominant groups define minorities, they are likely to compile a different list from one compiled by members of the groups so defined. The concept of the modern rational fixed identity has been extensively attacked, perhaps most effectively by Foucault and Derrida (Derrida, 1981; Foucault, 1979). Ali Rattansi is succinct:

> Identities,relationally and contingently formed, are constituted by power relations, and are always open to 'dislocation' and threatened by the 'outside' or 'other' which in part defines the positive elements. In effect, the social is a 'decentered structure' composed of practices of centring, the construction of power centres around nodal points of articulation (Rattansi, 1994a, p.31).

As a consequence of such processes, the definitions will differ from state to state, and the defining process *within* the state will differ according to specific circumstances, usually relating to the power relations between the groups concerned. Even international organisations' definitions are subject to similar forces. Obviously these relationships will change over time, leading to further redefinition, both by the groups themselves and those seeking to define them.

The most common result of such processes is the continual, changing definitions of group or minorities in terms of a particular set of socio-economic attributes. The most common of these are detailed in Fig.1.

As Figure 1 demonstrates, minorities can be of many types. People can classify themselves, or may be classified by others, in more than one of these categories, further adding to the complexity of describing identities within a modern state. The point is that minority groups can be of many types and to see them solely in terms of, say, an ethnic minority within a hostile state is too narrow a perspective. Thus, who actually does the defining is important. We can define ourselves and the groups to which we belong, in terms of language, history, culture, religion, history and so forth, but others may define us in different ways. They may only see our religious affiliations or our skin colour and define us in terms that suit their prejudices and stereotypes rather than our sense of ourselves and our group. This latter point is all important in education, as it is often a minority, the economically and politically powerful, who define the nature of the education that the state is to provide for its future citizens.

6.2. Education Systems and Differentiation

All European states maintain differentiated education systems. Such differentiation is a critical educational manifestation of a state's response to, amongst other things, multiculturalism and the demands of all types of minorities amongst its citizenry. A key element in this differentiation is the degree of either separation or segregation that the state allows within its education system. By separation is meant that minorities choose or have access to an appropriate form of detached educational provision and by segregation is meant that the state decides on the appropriate form of detached provision, with or without the consent of the minorities concerned. This can be made clearer if some of the models of differentiation adopted by education systems are examined. As Figure 2 indicates, such differentiation can be bewildering in terms of both number and type.

These levels of differentiation often overlap as in an elite Magyar grammar school in Transylvania, or in a home economics class for girls only in a Roman Catholic special school for children with moderate learning difficulties in Northern Ireland. It is clear that the range of potential differentiation is very large indeed. However, we need here to raise three issues that arise from the listing given in Figure 2. The first is to repeat that all European education systems differentiate. Whether this is a good or bad

Figure 1. The differentiation of minorities.

Economic
The rich in any state are a minority, but seldom one for whom concern is expressed in the terms of this book. Economic and educational disadvantage have repeatedly been shown to coincide. Successful policies to reduce or eliminate this coincidence have been appreciably less frequent.

Disability
People with disabilities are often stigmatised and discriminated against, particularly in education.

Religion
Religious minorities have often been persecuted in Europe and continue to be so.

Language
Linguistic minorities frequently have their language rights ignored by dominant linguistic groups.

Nationality
By this is meant a group who see themselves as a distinct people or nation within a larger state. They often have long established historical claims to territory within that state.

Refugees and asylum-seekers
These minorities, unlike the others, do not so much make legal claims upon the state to which they have fled, although of course they have them. Rather, they mainly appeal to larger international conventions for their limited minority rights.

'Race'
A meaningless term in science but with an erroneous commonsense meaning.

Ethnicity
Something of a catch all concept, meaning a group who see themselves and/or are seen by others as being a distinctive group within the state, through having certain attributes in common such as a common history, culture, language, religion and so forth. Into this category might come minority groups who are nomadic or who travel, for whom majority discrimination often seems focused on this particular aspect of their lives.

Figure 2. The differentiation of education

Education systems can be differentiated in some or all of the following ways:

By **wealth** — state or private educational institutions.

By **attainment** — elite educational institutions, such as grammar schools, lycees and gymnasia; adult and technical education as against universities.

By **gender** — separate schools or different curricula for boys and girls.

By **behaviour** — separate educational institutions or classes for pupils seen as disruptive or separate provision for those convicted of crime.

By **disability/special educational need** — 'special' educational institutions for pupils and students with disabilities that make it inappropriate, in the view of the education authorities, for them to be within mainstream educational institutions, classes or curricula.

By **location**
— there are frequently differences between educational institutions in prosperous and poor areas, even though both are funded by the state;
— educational institutions in rural or urban areas are again frequently different in their resourcing and curricula.

By **attendance**
— boarding/residential or day institutions.
— part-time or full time; daytime or evening.

By **religion** — religious educational institutions/secular educational institutions; also, different educational institutions for different religions within the one system.

By **language** — educational institutions using one national language and other educational institutions in the same system using another national language or other languages.

By **curricula** — for example in educational institutions with an agricultural, technical or other vocational specialism.

By **nationality** — although often seen in terms of religion and /or language, this category could apply to those educational institutions set up to educate refugee and asylum seeking students apart from the mainstream state system.

By **age** — compulsory, post-compulsory; adult and continuing education; education for the elderly.

By **contact.** — classroom or correspondence/radio/TV, distance learning.

By **'race'** — segregated educational institutions, both *de facto* and *de jure*.

state of affairs is beside the point: no system has, in practice, been able to avoid it.

Secondly, when differentiation is forced upon minorities, educational inequalities are a very likely consequence. Differentiation based upon separation also has its pitfalls, however. Although in principle desirable, minorities insisting upon a self-imposed form of educational segregation can, in certain cases, bring upon themselves undesirable educational outcomes. However, a true intercultural (and indeed, postmodern) educational system would, in general, favour minorities' rights to the forms of schooling they find appropriate to their needs. It is a dilemma that all European education systems have to face. Accept separation and the unity of the state may be threatened; enforce segregation and the unity of the state also may be threatened. There is no simple answer and each state usually attempts to resolve the issue in ways which best secure its own stability rather than the educational needs of the minorities concerned.

Moreover, the issue cannot be looked at merely at the state level, particularly in the current global context. With the Russian Federation stretching from the Polish border to the Chinese border, there is the further issue of regional groupings and the inclusions and exclusions that those imply. For example, if Russia is in Europe, are all members of the Russian Federation European? Recent Russian adventures in the Caucasus seem to suggest confusion in Moscow over the issue. Related issues are found all across the globe, as was discussed in Chapter Four. This means that the educational rights of minorities are not just the concern of individual states, but often have regional implication which are only recently being explored.

Thirdly, although education and training systems often treat minorities as if they were a homogenous group, minorities are themselves internally differentiated, segregated and separated, in education as in socio-economic life generally. This raises issues in relation to individual human rights vis-a-vis minority group rights. And as the 1993 Vienna meeting of the UN on Human Rights indicated, there is no agreement about the nature of the fundamental human rights on which, ultimately, group rights are predicated. The difficulty is that without such agreement, the educational rights of such groups are likely to become more difficult to assert.

Postmodernity's concern with differentiation and fracture is much less easy to advocate with regard to the structure of education systems than it is with regard to curriculum. The progressive, egalitarian position on the structure of educational systems has been the advocacy of the common school. The opposition to denominational schooling in France, the attempts to introduce desegregation in the United States and the movement to establish comprehensive schools in the UK have all had this aim in view. Opposition to private schooling, bi- and tri-partite systems, restricted access to higher education, special language classes, segregated special education similarly look to establish schools and universities which are open to all pupils and students and in which all can be educated side by side (Bash et al, 1985). At present, progress towards the common school seems to be in reverse in many countries of the European Union. The common school is undeniably an aspect of the Enlightenment project, despite the fact that modernity's insistence on hierarchy and stratification have made it difficult to achieve. This has resulted in the astonishing range of structural differentiation described above. But is not this differentiation precisely what postmodernity would celebrate? This issue is taken up by Andy Green (1994; see also Hargreaves, 1994) in a recent overview article:

> Postmodernism has little of value to offer educational theory but it has many dangers. The greatest of these is that the logic of the postmodern argument points towards an individualistic educational consumerism in many respects similar to that advocated by the free-marketeers of the new Right (p.76).

Whilst postmodernity's celebration of the thousand blooming flowers has much appeal when considering curricular systems in Europe it may be construed as anti-progressive by some of those concerned to establish the egalitarian common school.

What is at issue here may be two contrasting versions of difference. This book has so far concentrated on difference in demographic, cultural and curricular terms. It has seen difference, as the jargon has it, as something to be celebrated; certainly something to be identified, recognised and empowered. But another version of difference, derived from modernist psychology, stresses the differences between pupils and students in terms of their aptitudes and abilities. This version centres around intelligence as a fixed entity which can be applied to all mental tasks. This intelligence is seen as being differential between individuals and, in the extreme version, inherited. This version of intelligence has been vigorously opposed in the formal terms of psychology (Kamin, 1974; Evans and Waites 1981). It is a version of the human mind which is entirely at odds with the postmodern notion of the decentred self (Giddens, 1991). Nevertheless, this conception of intelligence is still a fundamental assumption of those trapped within the modernist programme, especially among those concerned with education.

It is this version of difference which Green identifies with the new Right. In terms of educational structure this version of difference has stressed choice and diversity of provision as a legitimation for the (re-) establishment of selective, hierarchical and elitist educational structures. Whilst Green is correct then in recognising that postmodern theory could be used by the new Right as a legitimation for their educational policies — though it is hard to imagine the personnel concerned being avid readers of Lyotard and Derrida — he is probably being unduly harsh in considering that such theory can only point in this direction. The new Right are seeking to re-establish the theories and structures of modernity, whether these be centralist curricula or differentiated educational structure.

This does not of course answer the implied question as to what sorts of educational structures would be congruent with postmodernist theories. Certainly Arnowitz and Giroux (1991) present a more optimistic possibility than that of Green. In both cases, however, the extrapolation from postmodern theory to educational practice is strained, though Green is correct to emphasise the tension between the progressive educational agenda and postmodernity's stress on fracture and difference. Postmodernity cannot axiomatically provide a progressive, reformist programme: it exists partly as the critique of all such programmes. To look to these theories for educational structural responses to diversity is to misunderstand their nature. The commitment to equality and the common school are one version of the project of modernity just as bi- and tri-partite systems are another version. In this respect Arnowitz and Giroux correctly conclude that:

> What is at stake here is the recognition that postmodernism provides educators with a more complex and insightful view of the relationships of culture, power and knowledge. But for all of its theoretical and political virtues, postmodernism is inadequate to the task of rewriting the emancipatory possibilities of the language and practice of revitalised democratic public life (Arnowitz and Giroux, 1991, p.81).

The debate on the appropriate form of educational structure is one within the discourse of modernity to which postmodern theory can only provide a ludic yet often irrelevant critique. Across Europe this debate within the modernist project of education has resulted in a dramatic and complex range of structural responses to diversity.

To help make this complexity of responses clearer, it is worth looking at one of the elements of differentiation in more detail. The issue of language is chosen both because it is one of the themes of this book and because it remains a constant issue for most education systems.

6.3. Educational Differentiation and Minority Languages

One of the critical ways in which minorities define themselves and/or are defined by others and/or are also discriminated against is through their language. This is not surprising as language is an essential part of identity, for individuals, for groups and for states. Language, defined here in its widest sense, is also seen as one of the bonds that holds a state together. It is therefore one of the most important functions of the education system to ensure that its young people are taught to be literate in the state language or languages. It is also important — although not all states would accept this — that young people should be literate in their first language or mother tongue when it is not a state language. Not surprisingly, this has meant that one of the most difficult issues in education is the language (or languages) of instruction. How state education systems respond to the languages of their minority group students is often a key test of how far the state responds to the more general needs of minorities (Skutnabb-Kangas, 1990). Nigel Grant, writing in Scots, puts this well, at the same time making a further point about linguistic acceptance:

> In the time o Franco, anerlie Castilian had onie status, an Catalan (an Galician, an Basque) wesnae permittit in the press or in the schule, aiven on the telephone an in public. A frien o mine yit minds, in his bairntime, speikin Catalan wi his faither on the bus, bein tellt bi a polis, 'Hey! Hable cristiano!' (Speik Christian.) Catalan hed nae place avaa, an the schules ettled tae turn the bairns oot aa Spaniards, an naethin else (Grant, 1993, p.1).

To put such debates in their context, however, it has to be admitted that for much of the modern period, languages have been disappearing at an ever-increasing rate. However, if contemporary language history shows that many languages are in decline and some becoming extinct, it also shows that other languages are growing, both in numbers and in dealing adequately with the vast explosion of knowledge that has characterised the last few centuries. An interesting example of this would be the increase in signing languages over the last hundred or so years. Another example would be English. Apart from its domination of commercial and financial discourses, of particular educational significance is the way in which English dominates scientific discourse: scientists who wish to be at the forefront of their area have to have access to the scientific journals, some eighty per cent of which are published in English. Similarly, much of the scientific discussion held via the Internet is also in English. This linguistic domination leads to many other issues. One would be the interesting fact that English speakers are usually cut off from journals and other scientific discourses in other languages, often not true the other way around.

Although languages like English may be growing, many others are not. This could be perceived in classic market philosophy terms; in other words, it could be argued that languages follow a path of linguistic Darwinism, leading to the survival of the fittest. In such a view, why should languages that fail to compete survive?

Such a question seems harsh but, as many languages continue to decline in terms of the number of speakers, it needs to be asked. Are not languages part of humanity's creative achievement that should be cherished? Particularly if the language is little used in a written form, is not the language of a minority group nonetheless its culture, its history, its identity? Furthermore, the loss of a language is also the loss of the way in which it was possible to be social, to be human:

> Human beings do not live in the objective world alone nor alone in the world of social activity as ordinarily understood, but are very much at the mercy of the particular language which has become the medium of expression for their society. It is quite an illusion to imagine that one adjusts to reality essentially without the use of language and that language is merely an incidental means of solving specific problems of communication or reflection. The fact of the matter is that the 'real

world' is unconsciously built up on the language habits of the group. ... We see and hear and otherwise experience largely as we do because the language habits of our community predispose certain choices of interpretation (Sapir, 1921 quoted in Hodge and Kress, 1993, p.62).

Over two hundred years ago, in 1773, Dr. Johnson told James Boswell that he was 'always sorry when any language is lost, because languages are the pedigrees of nations' (quoted in James Boswell's *Tour of the Hebrides* in the entry for 18 September, 1773). More recently, the Indian scholar, Professor D.P. Pattanayak, put it equally elegantly:

Many languages form a national mosaic. If some petals wither and fall off or some chips are displaced from the mosaic, then the lotus and the mosaic look ugly. With the death of languages, the country will be poorer (quoted in Skuttnabb-Kangas and Cummins, 1988, p.379).

Such views are powerful and long-standing and are increasingly accepted by many European governments, as the adoption, in 1992, of the Council of Europe's European Charter for Regional or Minority Languages indicates.

If the loss of a language is a diminution of our common humanity, a further answer to the linguistic Darwinists is that languages are not commodities. They are in competition of course, particularly whenever two or more languages are used within the same geographical, political, economic or cultural space. But competition does not axiomatically carry with it the concept of extinction. Winners and losers, perhaps, but loss, within a post-modern framework, does not of itself imply death, nor indeed, decline. The danger here is one of some form of linguistic determinism or monism. If a language is in decline, the argument goes, that decline will continue until it dies out. This is a simplistic view of linguistic change and is also empirically wrong. For example, the break-up of the Soviet Union has already led to a renewed revival of many former republic languages, which had been declining in terms of numbers of speakers and power under the Russian language dominated Soviet Union. Furthermore, in the new Baltic states, where Estonian, Lithuanian and Latvian are expanding, Russian is declining. Even the use of Russian as a second language is declining, as the case of the former Eastern Europe well illustrates. Casting off Soviet influence has often been followed by the replacement of Russian by English and/or German as second/third languages in the education systems. It has also led to the creation of new stigmatised minorities, the Russians. Interestingly, however, the Russian state's concern for Russians in other parts of the former Soviet Union is increasingly being couched in linguistic rather than ethnic terms (Higgins, 1994). This again argues against a simple economistic and monolingual view of language competition.

Thus, despite concern about the loss of languages, one of the fascinating facts about them is their powers of survival, despite their frequent neglect in education. Even in Western Europe, where state policies in education have often denied status and space to minority languages, they continue to survive and are slowly reappearing in both schools and universities. The apparently monolingual UK and France for example, contain over a dozen other so-called indigenous languages within their borders. The UK has Cornish, French, Irish Gaelic, Manx, Scottish, Scottish Gaelic and Welsh. France has Basque, Breton, Catalan, Corsican, Dutch, German and Occitan. The various sign languages used in both countries could also be added. Yet even this complex linguistic picture is far from the complete reality. There are, in addition, many hundreds of other languages spoken in Europe which have been introduced over the last hundred years or so as a consequence of the continuing migration of peoples into Europe. Many of these can legitimately lay claim to be European languages with equal rights to other languages in terms of their use in education. The linguistic diversity found within many of the major cities of Europe reflects a feature common to urban areas across the globe. For example, in London, over two hundred different languages are spoken by students in the education system, probably making it the most linguistically diverse city education system in the world (DES, 1980; ILEA, 1989). London is, of course, not unique. As cities grow in size and population, so they grow in linguistic and other diversities, all of which cause debate in their schooling and university systems. Cities like Paris and London for example, have some speech communities as large as any in their putative state of origin. A further example would be Melbourne, which, amongst other large linguistic groups, has the largest Greek speaking community after Athens.

Yet, as was discussed earlier in this chapter, language is one of the key ways in which people define themselves, the community to which they belong and in which they define people who do not belong. The rise in the power of the state over the last two centuries, particularly in the field of education, has been accompanied by a rise in the consciousness that language is a defining category as well as a means of communication (Lee, 1992). It is important to refute the simplistic view that by speaking the same language we help eliminate conflict: the civil wars that continue to take place around the world frequently refute that view. Even worse is the view that states contain few language minorities within their boundaries. The Australian example quoted earlier is particularly poignant, but there are many other examples of linguistically complex states such as Indonesia, Brazil, India and Nigeria. A reasonable guesstimate is that five thousand languages jostle for position in only two hundred or so states. The task facing European education systems is consequently a daunting one, as the spread of languages follows economic or political migration.

Yet, in everyday terms, the issue remains one of the nature and status of bilingualism or multilingualism in the schools and universities. At this point, it is important to stress that multilingualism is about *usage* not *competence*. In other words, a student is bilingual or multilingual if s/he has to operate in more than one language at any time rather than if s/he can speak, read and write more than one language at some arbitrary level. For many minority students, multilingualism often means *speaking* (rather than writing) more than one language, most frequently, one language at home and another language (or other languages) outside the home. Particularly in the case of education, this frequently means a different language at home from the one used in school or university.

Over the years, many linguists have drawn up taxonomies to describe the range of ways in which educational systems may deal with the issue of languages. Perhaps the most helpful for our purposes are those which stress not just the status and usage of languages but the purposes behind the policies (see, for example, Fishman, 1975 and Skutnabb-Kangas, 1990). If that is done, a somewhat similar set of potential perspectives can be seen to those often put forward in relation to societal responses to more general diversity, namely a range of policies on a continuum of 'assimilation to pluralism'. At one end, language policies are either monolingual or use other languages used by students mainly to ensure a smooth transition from them to the official language(s) used by the education system. Competence in the language of instruction having being acquired, the mother tongue or home language of the student is subsequently ignored or given solitary and separate subject status. As more multilingualism is allowed in the system, in speaking and in writing and in various parts of the curriculum, so greater linguistic pluralism is revealed. In the more pluralistic educational systems there will be encouragement for pupils and students who only speak the main state language to learn that of one of the minority groups. Again, as is so often the case in education, there is no one 'best way'. Institutions which are fully multilingual or bilingual are found across Europe but there are almost certainly far fewer than needed.

This discussion of language indicates that minority educational rights are difficult both to define and to meet in education systems. Greater interaction across Europe also means that a faster rate of evolution is taking place in communities' sense of themselves. But such interaction also points to an important question, both at the level of theory and of educational practice, namely the relationship between pluralism and assimilation. Debates about societal responses to diversity have a relatively brief history, often describing short periods of time, whereas the issues involved in relation to societal responses to diversity probably require examination over a far longer period. Educational institutions cannot be expected to resolve issues which few national governments have even considered. More pointedly, societies and their educational systems have to grapple with issues of demanding pluralisms within a European and global context of growing exclusion *and* assimilation. If there are assimilationist tendencies, educational differentiation can always be redefined in order to exclude and to dominate, in education as well as in the wider society. Furthermore, such tendencies can be reinforced by a whole range of other educational practice. In other words, education systems in Europe, as elsewhere, can, and often do, encourage assimilation and worse, ethnocentricism, narrow nationalism and chauvinism. They are, in the terms of this book, attempting to impose a discredited modernist framework on education systems. It is post-modern theories that give a purchase on the complex issues involved.

Chapter Seven

ETHNOCENTRICITY, POSTMODERNITY AND EUROPEAN KNOWLEDGE SYSTEMS

7.1. European Knowledge Systems and Ethnocentricity

Education systems mediate ethnocentrism. They can seek to reduce ethnocentrism; they can choose to ignore it as an issue and certainly in this way do nothing to reduce it; or they can actually enhance it. The ways in which ethnocentricity and discrimination can be enhanced or reduced through the structures and policies of education systems have become familiar. On the one hand, special schools and strands, segregated language classes, private and denominational schools, standardised ethnocentric testing related to repetition, streaming or to differentiated schools are structural policies whereby discrimination and ethnocentrism may be reproduced and enhanced (Bash, et al 1985). On the other hand, integration, equal opportunities policies, the creation or preservation of the common school, positive discrimination and higher education quota systems are policies whereby systems can attempt to reduce and eliminate discrimination and ethnocentricity (Arora and Duncan, (eds) 1986).

This chapter examines one theme of education policy, which is actually critical to the production, reproduction or elimination of ethnocentrism, namely the curricula of schools and higher education institutions. It is a contention of this book that the presence of ethnocentricity in Europe is crucially connected to what is often taught in educational institutions. It is the curricular systems of Europe which frequently generate and reproduce much of this ethnocentricity. Curricular systems may give particular versions of regional, national and European history. They may stress the importance of regional and national languages and canons of literature. They may present a particular view of the development of mathematics, science, engineering and medicine. They may privilege the artistic, cultural and scientific products of particular cities, regions and nations. The ways in which all this may be done are manifold, ranging from the presentation of European history in the compulsory textbooks used in Greece, through the deification of Shakespeare in literary discourse in the UK, to the conception of science and mathematics as exclusively European creations which is general in universities across the European Union.

If this contention is correct, it has profound implications for the future harmony of the European Union and for that very widening and deepening to which it is committed. Within the state-funded institutions of the countries of the Union, materials are being taught which, far from assisting in the processes of widening and deepening, are likely to influence pupils, students and future populations adversely. Ethnocentricity is a major content of school and university curricula.

If this were a matter of rival versions of knowledge embedded in the curricular systems of the member states of the Union, it would be serious enough. But what is in danger of emerging is a consensus of knowledge between the states of the Union which is all the more ethnocentric for presenting itself as pan-European. Even such a commentator as Smith can envisage the emergence of a common European culture:

> Though the will to co-operation among European states is mainly economic in content, it is also based on cultural assumptions and traditions. ... there are also broader European cultural patterns which transcend national cultural boundaries to create an overlapping 'family' of common components. Democratic ideals and parliamentary institutions; civil rights and legal codes; Judeo- Christian traditions of ethics; the values of scientific enquiry; artistic traditions of realism and romanticism; humanism and individualism: these are some of the cultural patterns which straddle many of Europe's national cultures, to create a syndrome of repeated elements and form a culture area of overlapping components (Smith, 1990, p.187).

Notice that in the attempt to visualise a European culture two processes have taken place. Firstly, only the positive elements of European history and culture are presented. Secondly, many of the progressive elements in the history and culture of the wider world are expropriated into an exclusively European entity.

The emergence of the European supernationality has important repercussions in epistemological and curricular terms. (The issue of curricular harmonisation is further examined in Chapter Eight.) As political and economic power becomes concentrated in the Union — a union of states — then scientific exactitude, cultural achievement, moral rightness, historical destiny are also being perceived to be the accomplishment of these fifteen states. The elitist claims of European culture and knowledge are now being embodied in a political and economic superpower located in one geographical section of the continent. As these notions of culture and knowledge become embedded in curricular systems, through the process of Europeanisation, the ethnocentric implications of the pan-European curriculum are all too easily overlooked.

Before offering any more complex taxonomy, it is worth considering those groups of people and those contributions to human knowledge which are overlooked, disparaged or plagiarised by European curricular systems. Three brief examples may be offered: firstly, non-majority indigenous groups within a particular state or states of the Union; secondly, first and second generation migrants and their families who, with their own knowledge and cultures embodied in their traditions, have often settled in the centres of the large cities of the Union; thirdly, those countries on the periphery of the Union whose status as European is increasingly marginalised. Each of these examples is considered in turn.

Non-majority groups in several of the states of the Union have achieved greater visibility for themselves in the post-war period: Catalans, Welsh, Bretons. The countries of the European Union are regionalising with differing degrees of enthusiasm. Catalonia now enjoys an autonomy that many Scots or Corsicans would envy. Regionalisation within the European Union has proved economically as well as politically successful. For many the principle of subsidiarity relates not to states but to regions. The European Union would then devolve power to its regions leaving the states as outmoded anachronisms to wither on the bough (Harvie, 1994). The Europeanisation of the curriculum, with its inevitable stress on the approved state languages of the European Union, may threaten this shift of control to the regions and with it the very existence of their languages, cultures and traditions.

Secondly, those groups, which, for lack of a more acceptable terminology, we follow European Union practice in referring to as migrant, represent a great range of the cultures (and knowledge systems) of the world: Magrhebians in Paris, Turks in Frankfurt, Surinamese in Rotterdam, Bangladeshis in East London or West Africans in Naples (Noin and Woods, (eds) 1993). Despite the presence of these groups, their languages and the cultural and knowledge systems of the entire continents of Africa and Asia are almost entirely neglected in European curricular systems.

Thirdly and finally, Europe itself is being redefined within the Union as the fifteen rich member states. The countries of Central and Eastern Europe and the former constituent states of the Soviet Union are seen increasingly as marginal. They are seen not only as marginal to the economic power of the Union, their contribution to European knowledge, history and culture is also being marginalised. They are beyond the pale of the mighty European civilisation. This perception is felt most keenly in the Balkan countries (Gillwald et al 1992). The civil war in the former Yugoslavia is both the product of ethnocentrism in that region and a potential cause of it in the European Union.

This chapter follows Chapter Four in suggesting that European curricular systems can be categorised into three broad types: traditional, modern and postmodern. The taxonomy offered here analyses ways in which systems of knowledge in schools and universities can reproduce or erode ethnocentrism. Traditional, modern and post-modern are obviously terms which imply chronology. However, whilst in the broadest of terms this may seem to be the case, in the instance of curricular analysis the three categories have not been successive. Rather, as was shown in Chapter Four, protagonists of each of these three versions of knowledge may be seen to be in conflict over the definition of the school and university curriculum in many of the member states of the European Union. (McLean, 1990 offers a radically different assessment of European curricular systems to that presented in this chapter.) The three terms then represent, rather than a chronological process, ideologies and forces within the politics of curriculum planning at the various levels at which these are conducted.

7.2. Traditional and Modern Knowledge Systems in the School and University Curriculum

Traditional knowledge systems based around religious belief, the centrality of the family and notions of group or national supremacy have not entirely disappeared from the curricula of schools and universities either within or beyond the European Union (see Chapter Four for references). The persistence of denominational schooling in the Netherlands and the UK and its re-emergence in France are structural manifestations of this. Even in higher education, some of the most prominent universities of the Union remain denominational in character. Despite its many strengths and remarkable persistence, among the curricular concomitants of this form of education are stereotypical gender and family pattern expectations, religious intolerance, homophobia, and often xenophobia.

Traditional knowledge systems endorse and seek to propagate the civilisation its protagonists consider to have been established within their culture (whether politically or geographically defined) and, effectively, nowhere else. They point to the achievements of specific European nations or cities as the whole of human civilisation. This civilisation or culture is conceptualised in terms of particular activities and particular outstanding proponents (almost all of them men). Philosophy begins with Plato and Aristotle. After the Renaissance its canon is almost exclusively defined from men writing in German, French or English. Architectural achievements are those of the Athenian Acropolis, the Gothic cathedrals or Renaissance Florence. Literature is seen as an agreed canon of classic texts with, in England, an overwhelming stress on Shakespeare, and similar but not perhaps equal pre-eminences in other states, on Cervantes, Goethe, Dante, Racine, Christian Andersen, Burns. Both religious and secular music are seen to be largely the product of a very few states. Art and sculpture reach their triumphal period in the Italian Renaissance when Brunelleschi, Raphael, Alberti and so on rediscovered the perfections of Athenian form. Within traditional knowledge systems scientific and technological activities are less valued then in modern systems, though attention will be paid to the activities of particular national heroes, Henry the Navigator, Newton, Bohr.

Since this traditional version of European knowledge has been and remains so influential on both the form and content of educational systems, it may be worth spelling out some of the major questions that it raises. Why was traditional knowledge created almost exclusively by men? Why did it occur on just one continent? Why is easel painting given so much importance as against road building or town planning? Why is composing concerti seen as more important than draining swamps or designing factory systems? Why is this knowledge system so conflict-free?

In fact the traditionalist is a sexist and imperialistic view of European knowledge. Even in the elitist terms of culture which it seeks to establish, it draws only on a grotesquely impoverished canon. It is ethnocentric in its core and formation. The voices which it excludes are actually those which offer it any possibility of greater depth. It is necessary to isolate and question it because it retains such power in both curricular systems and, not unconnectedly, the way in which groups of people organise their political beliefs. For various groups, in various states, it can easily be interpreted as the triumph of Catholicism or the triumph of Protestantism, as the central role in global civilisation of a particular state, be it as small and insignificant as Portugal, Holland or England. It provides a cultural and political underpinning for existing political and economic relations. It conceals relations of social and economic dominance both within states and between them. It endorses class relationships and international patterns of exploitation as the only viable, right and happy order of things. It is only non-contested because so many groups can contribute their own petty chauvinisms to the overall imperialism which perceives human history as *The Triumph of the West* (Roberts, 1980).

Turning to modernist knowledge systems, these are connected to a wider programme in education which can be identified in the European Union and beyond. As suggested in earlier chapters, this programme is an aspect of the wider Enlightenment or modernist project (Harvey, 1989). In educational terms this programme consists of a set of beliefs and assumptions which were, and to some extent still are, widely held and a range of policies which were implemented and endorsed without eliminating political and ideological difference. Five of the elements of this programme may be identified as relating to European knowledge systems. Firstly, there is a belief in the ineluctable progress towards the ever greater acquisition and accuracy of human knowledge. Secondly, it is overwhelmingly science which is seen as both the true method and the important subject matter of knowledge. Thirdly, there is an assumption of technical or professional relevance within this knowledge system: it aspires not only towards truth but towards usefulness, ultimately towards effectiveness in the place of work or the place of warfare. Fourthly, there is a strange lack of contention regarding the subject matter and organisation of the school and university curriculum: academic subjects are taken at face value and their artificial division of knowledge as epistemologically and pragmatically valid. Fifthly, it is assumed that human beings will have different ranges of access to this knowledge: this may depend upon their social class, gender, culture or (compounding and legitimating these categories) perceived intelligence. This modernist knowledge system has been so taken for granted at various points as to be hardly identifiable as such. In particular it is fundamental to curricular systems which have functioned to reproduce not only its content but also its uncontested supremacy.

Although it may be seen as part of a wider Enlightenment project, the reasons for identifying this system as modernist is not simply to do with the historical period in which its ideals were proposed and legitimated. The modernist system is a holistic and progressive project. It aspires towards progressive and general social betterment. It is informed by liberal political ideals and relates to other dimensions of the liberal and modernist programmatic. It is linked to a belief in humane knowledge on the one hand and technological progress on the other. It has largely been implemented through bureaucratic institution-building and credibility in professional competence. It is underpinned by stratified conceptions of human personality and ability and by hierarchical modes of organising knowledge.

Each part of the modernist system relates coherently to other constituent parts. At a theoretical level a psychology which stresses individual difference and which centres itself on the notion of intelligence integrates readily with a society and a workplace which depend on mechanisms of stratification and control. These are further congruent with an elitist education system characterised by frequent national testing. Similarly, an epistemology which sees knowledge in subject terms and these subjects as stratified by status, relevance or importance may readily be related in both theoretical and educational institutional ways to elitist psychology and stratified social and economic systems. The illusion of organic unity between theories and between theory and policy is key to the holistic modernist project.

It is within this illusion of unity and holism that the danger of ethnocentricity is most obvious within the modernist knowledge system. It is an epistemology that allows for only one science or number system and in extreme cases for only one scientific method (Popper, 1972; Feyerabend, 1978a; 1978b). The knowledges and cultures of non-dominant groups in terms of political, economic and academic power are devalued and dismissed.

This holism becomes even more potentially ethnocentric once it is amplified through the self-confident supernationality of the European Union. Modernist knowledge is perceived as the product of Europe (now implicitly meaning the European Union) and perhaps, more recently, its academic annex, the USA. As Europe is increasingly unified, so its knowledge system can become ever more holistic, powerful and exclusive. The modernist European knowledge system, just as much as the traditional knowledge system is ethnocentric in its definition. When transformed into curricular systems its effect can only strengthen and reproduce ethnocentricity and xenophobia.

7.3. Postmodern Knowledge as Critique: Cultural Relativism

The fractures in the edifices of traditional and modernist knowledge systems have come from the critiques which have been made in terms of class, gender, culture, religion or sexual orientation (see Chapter Four). Those groups who have seen their modes of knowledge acquisition, their forms of science, worship or family organisation as being devalued by the Enlightenment project have eventually succeeded in revealing the paucity of the modernist knowledge system. One example of this critique, which is fundamental to the issue of ethnocentrism is offered here. It is taken from the position of cultural relativism (and partially derived from an earlier paper on that theme, Coulby, 1993).

In considering the formation of European curricula there are at least two relevant issues derived from work on cultural relativism. The first, specifically European issue is the debate concerning the origins of European knowledge. The second, more general issue, concerns the value and validity that is placed upon the specific products and activities of one culture as against those of another.

Bernal challenges the Hellenistic inheritance on which modernist knowledge systems would claim to be founded. In the first volume of *Black Athena* (Bernal, 1987; see also Bernal, 1991), he attempts to overthrow accepted assumptions about the linguistic and cultural origins of Hellenic civilisation. In particular he is concerned to highlight the importance of Egyptian and Phoenician influences on the Greeks. He suggests that the Ancient Model of classical development, derived from the ancient Greek writers themselves, fully acknowledged the importance of Egypt and Phoenicia in the formation of Greek civilisation but that this model was overthrown by the Enlightenment and is currently discredited. As part of this argument he shows how, during the nineteenth century, first Egyptian and then Phoenician influences on Hellenic civilisation were systematically undervalued and denied in the writing of the major European classicists. Bernal is able to link convincingly this shift in classical scholarship to shifting attitudes in the nineteenth century firstly towards Egypt and to Africa generally and secondly towards the Jews.

The Ancient Model fell not because of any new developments in the field but because it did not fit the prevailing world-view. To be more precise, it was incompatible with the paradigms of race and progress of the early 19th century (Bernal, 1987 p.316).

The obvious importance of Bernal's argument to this book is that it brings into question the origins of that civilisation from which most Europeans believe their knowledge and culture to have derived. Within the emergent super-power of the European Union, there is a growing awareness of and stress on the common origins of the continent's civilisation. This may be presented in the simplistic historical continuum: Greece, Rome, Christianity, Renaissance, Enlightenment, Modern Science. Human civilisation is seen as white, Western and European. Bernal raises the question that the founding European civilisation might have been far from indigenous; that it might have owed many of its important and characteristic features to previous civilisations in Africa and Asia; that these civilisations might well have colonised the Greek mainland; and that Athena, goddess of wisdom and patroness of the founding city of Europe, was black.

Bernal makes clear the extent to which nineteenth century classicists were unwilling to accept non-European influences on the origins of Greece and thus on the continents's knowledge and culture. This tendency to

modernistic European knowledge system, then this has implications for the nature of the knowledge of the next generation of European citizens and of the society which they will create. It is necessary, then, to emphasise that no country in Europe consists of only one culture and that ethnocentrism and Eurocentrism will be hazardous traits for schools to encourage in the next generation both in terms of civil understanding and harmony within countries and in terms of the European Union's relationships with the rest of the world.

7.4. The Curricular Possibilities of Postmodernism

Whilst a post-modernist curriculum is hardly identifiable in any country of the European Union, the knowledge system on which it might be based has already emerged. Post-modernist knowledge sees Europe and its cities as part of a global system since before the rise of Knossos. It draws attention to the great periods and achievements of the wider interactions of European cities and states: Macedonia's contact with Persian culture, the influence of Eastern religions and moralities, the economic and cultural interchange between Venice and the East, the Arabic continuation of classical mathematics, science and philosophy, the tolerance and economic vitality of the Cordoba Caliphate. Post-modernist knowledge systems acknowledge not only the international contribution to European civilisation but also that European knowledge systems themselves must be placed within an international context of which Europe is but a part.

Post-modern knowledge systems recognise the importance of women in the formation of history, culture and knowledge. They recognise the wealth of different knowledges, sciences and cultures which are in dialogue and conflict. Such systems are intrinsically international in a way in which European traditional and modernist systems have failed to be.

Post-modernist knowledge systems acknowledge that the demographic pattern of the continent has been in ceaseless flux and that this flux can no more be stopped by the Treaty of Versailles than it could be by Offa's Dyke. The populations and boundaries of Europe can never be finalised. The continent has to find ways of adapting to this fact which go beyond fighting to the death to revise the last agreed boundary change but two.

This form of knowledge recognises that the achievements of the continent are multi-faceted and go far beyond easel painting to scientific, economic, social and familial practices. It insists that all these achievements were and continue to be influenced by practices and people beyond the boundaries of Europe; that interchange with Africa and Asia have been vital elements in the economic and cultural growth of Europe. Further, it refuses to have a view of Europe which is constrained by the boundaries of the European Union. The influences of Central and Eastern Europe cannot be separated from what has historically, culturally or scientifically been achieved by the continent. Post-modernist knowledge recognises that people from beyond Europe have, across many centuries, come to live in its towns and cities and that their contributions have been an invigorating element in urban economic and artistic success. Similarly, demographic interchange between the states and cities of Europe has played a vital part in its achievements.

It would be wrong to provide an alternative list of famous protagonists, since this view of knowledge does not see it as the achievement of a small group of heroes; rather it is the product of groups of women and men working together and in conflict over time. Nor can post-modernist modes of knowledge choose to remain oblivious to the fact that the interchanges within and beyond Europe were most often the result, in the first instance, of exploitation and conflict. Demographic movement in Europe has so often resulted from exploitation, imperialism and war. However, this paradigm insists that the real culture of Europe is the product of the heterogeneities generated by these movements and not some reified conflict-free art gallery or opera house.

With the resurgence of nationalism, xenophobia and ethnocentrism in both Eastern and Western Europe, finding ways in which social institutions can combat these forces may become a matter of the survival of the European democracies. Already there is racial war on the borders of the European Union. Peace, the continent was advised during the Spanish Civil War, is indivisible. At that point the advice was ignored.

School and university knowledge are vital elements in the reproduction of ethnocentrism. It is possible that they could be just as powerful elements in its reversal and ultimate elimination. But if they are to take on this role then it is critical that they do not retreat into traditionalist modes of knowledge (as the United Kingdom appears to be in the National Curriculum). Similarly, the privileging of western science and the modernist agenda of which it is such an important component, can only lead to a triumphalist version of Western Europe and its knowledge. This would play no part in generating harmony within the states of Europe, between the states of Europe or between Europe and the wider world. The postmodernist critique and its version of a pluralistic, contested, manifold, provisional knowledge may offer the most positive alternative for curricular systems. It may also help pupils and students achieve an understanding closer to the realities of the world in which they live.

At least one writer has linked postmodernity and education for a sustainable future more closely than this (Orr, 1992; 1993). For Orr the 'postmodern world' consists not of delicate and erudite theorising but of all too tangible difficulties which will confront pupils and students now in the education system as they come to adulthood in the twenty-first century. Some of these difficulties, such as the widening gap in incomes between the rich and poor worlds, are already current. Others are increasingly evident: the impending exhaustion of finite resources, especially carboniferous fuels; rapid, but differentially distributed, demographic expansion; erosion of agricultural and forest lands with associated irreversible reductions in the global genetic pattern; pollution of rivers, seas and oceans leading to destruction of animal and fish species and the erosion of food supplies; global warming and the destruction of the ozone layer with potential effects on both the sea-level and the viability of many plant and animal life forms; pharmaceutical exhaustion — for example of antibiotics — combined with rapid mutations on the part of viruses and infection-carrying insects.

This catalogue of potential disaster cannot be dismissed as merely millennial gloom. It seems that governments prefer to ignore these futures, engaging in huge road building schemes, for instance, to accommodate a mode of transport, the potential viability of which in terms of time scale is so severely limited. On the other hand it may be that governments are desperately aware of these constraints. The Gulf War provides an example of nightmarish ecological conflict as the small and static proportion of the world's population which owns the wealth and the armaments uses its power to take control of the crucial and diminishing resources, irrespective of the consequences for the rest of the world or for the ecosystem. But not only governments but also schools and universities are selective with regard to which aspect of the future they choose. If the population of the twenty-first century is to have the knowledge and skills firstly to recognise and then to combat these difficulties, they need to be educated for these tasks now.

Yet many of these issues are all but invisible in the school and university curricula of Europe. Crucially, the science taught is that which generated many of the difficulties listed above and which can only continue to exacerbate them (see Chapter Four). It is more than this: schools and universities continue to teach science as if it offered the solution to life's difficulties rather than contributing to their exacerbation. The teachers and scientists prepared even to acknowledge any of the potential disasters listed above all too often turn to science and technology for solutions. To return to the theme of oil, they look for more fuel-efficient internal combustion engines, or, more radically, to improved means of public transport. It is possible that these technical solutions will not suffice and that what is need is a massive reduction in mobility. Society will need to be reorganised so that people do not travel the distances typified by the average European lifetime. Enlightenment science has brought humanity to the brink of disaster but it is not Enlightenment science which can find the way back.

Once the 'postmodern world' is seen in these terms, the educational implications are profound indeed. Again they are crucially concerned with the construction and legitimation of curricular knowledge. If the teaching of science, technology and geography were to recognise some of the impending difficulties, it would go some way towards generating some of the skills which might lead to solutions. But more than this is required: science needs to be relativised and dethroned from its position as the solution rather the origin of humanity's difficulties. This involves a more sceptical, critical and relativistic approach to science than is current in European curricular systems but one which is consistent with the theoretical insights derived from postmodernity. In other subjects than science the skills of scepticism, critical thinking and relativistic knowledge will need to take a central place in the school and university curriculum.

Chapter Eight

NEW, OR MAKING THE SAME MISTAKES? RACISM, REFUGEES AND INTERCULTURAL EDUCATION IN EUROPE

8.1. Progressive Taxonomies and Oscillating Policies

This book argues that disillusion over the Enlightenment or modern agenda is neither new nor appropriate to education or to social life generally. It has argued that the late modern or postmodern agenda is not a paradigm shift, but more a careful reconsideration of the complexities involved in organising modern society. From its inception, this modern agenda has been opposed by forces of reaction, by religious funda- mentalism and by artistic movements of rejection, such as the Romantic movement in art, music and literature. The modern agenda appeared to triumph in the nineteenth century in much of Europe but its too-mechanistic underpinnings were already crumbling. Both in science and the arts, voices of criticism began to be increasingly heard and their arguments accepted. Relativity and subjectivity became recognised as being aspects of the modern agenda, although not without considerable social turmoil. The modern or late modern agenda seems to have incorporated the postmodernist critique as well as the more vociferous traditionalist counter-Enlightenment without being funda-mentally impaired or impeded. However, many existing modernist structures have proved incapable of meeting the new demands placed upon them by these changes, of which perhaps the most important is the modern state and, the major concern of this book, the state's educational system.

whether or not from minorities and/or disadvantaged groups. However, how the state defines such diversity can rarely be disputed within the education system save at the margins of educational practice. In other words, state education systems cannot be major elements for facilitating reform or change unless the government of the day wishes it, although they do maintain a degree of relative autonomy. Of course, states with forms of regional or local devolution for education may attempt to introduce practices in relation to diversity which differ from those of the central government. However, with few exceptions, educational policy and practice at regional and local levels is seldom dramatically opposed to the policy orientations of the central state. But there will be exceptions and there will be policy change. For example, educational policy and practice may be assimilationist in some parts of the system and more pluralistic in others. In states with politically significant minorities, or with highly devolved federal structures, educational practice may vary considerably between regions. Indeed, such change can occur within a single institution, reflecting individual teacher's mind-sets about diversity.

Such policy change was seldom recognised until the 1980s. Educational policy on social diversity in many education systems in Europe appeared, in the main, to follow the Street-Porter model. There appeared to be a slow move in general social policy, and in educational policy in particular, towards an acceptance of certain (and varied) aspects of pluralism. Also an acknowledgement of the discriminatory practices (for example sexism, racism, discrimination against people on religious or linguistic grounds or perceptions of disability) in the wider society that schooling was doing all too little to prevent. It was not a steady movement towards a more open and plural educational climate. Indeed, much educational policy in European Union states has remained discriminatory in practice.

However, from the 1980s onwards, the effects of what this book has called postmodernity has dramatically changed perspectives on educational (and other) responses to diversity. The break-down in confidence in the modern agenda has been as profound in education as elsewhere, as the complex consequences of modernity have become more apparent. As Bauman notes:

Postmodernity may be conceived of as a modernity conscious of its true nature — *modernity for itself*. The most conspicuous features of the postmodern condition: institutionalised pluralism, variety, contingency and ambivalence have all been turned out by modern society in ever increasing volumes; yet they were seen as signs of failure rather than success... (Bauman, 1992, pp.187-8).

There are two significant responses to this change in the perception of the modern agenda: the rise of fundamentalism in many major religions and the increase in nationalism. When accompanied by a greater expression of feelings of group exclusion and particularism rather than pluralism, this has led to dramatic changes in education for diversity in many states and to rapid policy change. One possible consequence of these sorts of changes is that educational policy can appear even more internally inconsistent than usual, extolling certain national and/or religious aspirations in the schools, while at the same time attempting to foster tolerance and resist xenophobia.

Policy change also relates to *levels* of administrative authority within a state's educational system. Many states are seeking to decentralise certain aspects of administrative policy on education, although most states still attempt to maintain control over key aspects of educational practice, most noticeably the curriculum, teacher education and university admissions and funding. Such decentralisation can often be intended to meet minority demands for greater control of their educational futures, although few states are yet prepared to move beyond the educationally less significant. However, devolution of policy authority poses grave questions for national level policy makers. Accept devolution and the unity of the state may be threatened, not just its education system; enforce central control and the unity of the state may also be threatened if minorities feel that their rights and aspirations, in education as elsewhere, are not being met or are being infringed. There is no simple answer to this issue and each state usually attempts to resolve it in ways which best secure the stability of the state rather than the educational needs of the minorities concerned.

A similar set of issues relate to the financing of special provision for minorities within a national system of education. In general, much financial policy in respect of minorities more usually reflects the political power or potential political power of minority and/or disadvantaged group in question. Minorities *per se* may have political power, particularly if they are affluent and can make tactical arrangements with other minorities. More usually, however, it means that generally disadvantaged groups are also educationally disadvantaged. Many governments do attempt to provide special provision for minority groups, particularly concerning language and access, but such funding is seldom seen as a core element in educational budgets. To complicate the issue further, funding policies, like educational policies generally, have to be looked at against a backcloth of community concern. In other words, have the educational policies proposed (or implemented) got the support of the minority and/or disadvantaged groups involved? Which raises a further set of issues in relation to group representation and legitimation. Educational policy makers would generally prefer to formulate, adopt and implement policies that meet the needs and have the approval of the minority groups concerned. In practice this rarely happens, for complex reasons. Some of these would be inherent in the process of educational policy formulation, adoption and implementation, some in the conflicts and misunderstandings that arise between elected politicians, appointed officials and minority opinion and its representatives. And as the policy makers fiddle, the Rome of minority educational aspiration continues to burn.

8.2. 'Owing to Well Founded Fear of Being Persecuted'

Nowhere are these issues brought to a head more clearly than in relation to the education of refugee children. Issues of class, sexual, ethnic and racial identity are to the forefront. The refugee groups are also outside the boundaries of the state, in a sense, living condemnations of the modern state's inability to meet the needs of its citizenry. Frequently they are comprehensively stigmatised. Yet far from being seen as indicators of the failure of the modern state to adapt more quickly to the complex realities of the postmodern agenda, they are seen as a temporary and regrettable phenomenon. Despite the pluralistic rhetoric, the policy across Europe is still mainly to put them into language classes so that they can quickly be given the tools to succeed in their new schooling system.

Moreover, refugee children are seen not merely as a temporary phenomenon but also as a new one — an equally fallacious view. Refugees provoke questions for all European Union states and schooling systems, which have to be resolved if all children are to be adequately educated and prepared for life in the twenty first century.

Refugees are a specific group of migrants, although the case could be made for saying that most migrants are refugees of one sort or another. Shortly after the Second World War, when Europe experienced large movements of refugees, the United Nations (UN) defined a refugee as a person who has left his/her own country 'owing to a well-founded fear of being persecuted for reasons of race, religion, nationality, membership of a particular social group or political opinion' (United Nations, 1951). A person thus defined, who has crossed an international border and is seeking formal refugee status is an asylum seeker. All members of the United Nations have subscribed to this Convention; this means that they accept the definition. How it is actualised is the concern of the individual state, for there is no effective monitoring of practice by the UN or its agencies. Thus, how a state deals with asylum seekers and gives or withholds refugee status is the concern of that state rather than of any international agency like the UN or its specialist offshoot, the United Nations High Commission for Refugees (UNHCR).

One major consequence of this state by state implementation is a wide variety of practice between states and also within states over time, the latter usually owing to varying internal political views currently held about particular groups of refugees. In Europe, examples of this would be the differential responses to Jewish refugees during the first half of this century and, later, to ex-colonial refugees.

Despite these difficulties, the United Nations convention gives a helpful operational definition which is widely used and which is sufficiently loose as to cover most cases of what many people would consider asylum seeking. However, although the United Nations definition is helpful, it needs to be placed in its context, particularly as it is related to the broader issue of the movement and settlement of people in Europe. Put as a question: are most migrants refugees of some sort — the so-called economic refugee — or are refugees a special kind of migrant deserving particular attention? More specifically, should educational practice change according to how groups of children in schools are defined by the state in which they reside? For, as the first section of this chapter indicated, states can define minorities in and out of existence according to the political needs of the moment. More often than not, the definitions that states adopt help to sustain a climate of marginalisation. As a result, each state in Europe defines its migrant/refugee population in subtly different ways, usually as a consequence of differing histories of settlement, of definition of citizenship and differing traditions in the social sciences that examine these phenomena. Attempts to standardise migration statistics are being made, most notably by the Statistical Division of the UN Economic Commission for Europe and the Statistical Office of the European Union. However, progress is slow and the current unsatisfactory position is likely to continue for some time.

The exact legal position in relation to European Union policy remains clouded by the uncertainty over the implementation of the Maastricht Treaty. What the treaty says in relation to asylum seekers and other migrants is well-intentioned but vague. The vagueness conceals more than it reveals. What is clear in practice is that the European Union is terrified by the refugee issue and is doing all in its power to restrict the flow of refugees across its borders. It is almost as if there has been a sudden realisation that the Iron Curtain was actually beneficial because it kept people out, rather than oppressive for keeping people in.

Attempts at European Union harmonisation over issues relating to refugees are likely to be resolved within this decade; discussions about refugees at the intergovernmental level are largely being placed in the more general context of policy in respect of all migration. As a result, the debates about refugees and refugee communities in the states of the European Union too often co-exist with debates dominated by xenophobia and racism, leading to a concern that the state solutions will be exclusion, as happened to Jewish refugees in the 1930s.

Countering such xenophobia is clearly a task for education systems, as discussed later in this chapter. But appropriate educational action, like more general social policy, depends partly on accurate information about the issue. Surprisingly, the statistical position regarding refugees in the states of the European Union is as confused as their other data on migration. There is still little data available about migration in the European Union. Such data is difficult to collect, although most European Union states do try to do so. It is also difficult to compare cross-nationally, given differences in definitions and data-collection categories. An added complication is that because some forms of migration are seen as illegal by the receiving country, the data collected may considerably underestimate the number of people actually involved. In particular, migration into Europe of people traditionally seen as 'non-European', whether as asylum seekers or as economic refugees, has been a major focus of socio-political concern, and this has affected education.

Post-war migration in Europe has different and significant strands. The within-state pattern of the migration of people from rural to urban areas is perhaps the most significant in numbers and in social policy terms, although it seldom impinges directly upon educational practice. However, the key issue about such patterns is that, although long term trends such as the rural-urban drift seem settled, the one certain thing about demographic change is that it is unpredictable. Change can take place far faster than state social policy can deal with it, as current East-West movements clearly demonstrate. Furthermore, general European trends, as opposed to national ones, are even more slowly determined by those responsible for social statistics. Their details, if disseminated at all, seldom have a wide audience. This is a particular cause for concern at a time of increasing confusion about the nature, purpose and implementation of greater European cohesiveness.

The national debates about diversity, particularly in relation to international in-migration, seldom looked at this aspect of migration in conjunction with other migratory patterns, which had surface similarities but often very different dynamics and participants. Thus, use of the term migration in Europe has now become a code for a specific type of migration, namely international migration, and the term migrant has become synonomous with the ideological construct of 'non-European'(see Chapter Three). Thus, individual states have to work out the nature and composition of their individual citizenries within an international 'European' context which offers them little useful guidance and much prejudiced opinion.

Given all this, how does the migratory picture look in the 1990s compared to the end of the 1980s? The most significant long term pattern, from the rural to the urban, from the agricultural to the industrial and service sectors, continues. International migration into Europe is now mainly family re-unification, alongside a small number of refugees from other parts of the world. Migration within Europe no longer reveals a South to North movement.

What is arousing current educational concern and the concern of policy makers in Europe generally, are the refugee movements. These movements have to be put in their international perspective. Refugees are a world-wide issue, with the overwhelming majority never reaching Europe. It is estimated that only six per cent of asylum seekers come to Europe (Rutter, 1994). The vast majority are in countries that are already poor and which have few resources to deal adequately with refugee needs. Yet many Europeans feel, quite incorrectly, that a flood of asylum seekers is beating on the collective European door. They err also in seeing asylum seekers as having the same aspirations as earlier groups of migrants who moved for more obvious economic reasons. This is not so. The so-called 'myth of return' is less likely to be a myth in relation to refugees, as many of the millions of refugees around the world will very likely return to the state they left , as and when that becomes possible. A small but interesting example is that of some four thousand Basque children who were sent to the UK to escape the horrors of the Spanish Civil War in 1937. Despite that war and the World War that followed, the majority returned home, only about four hundred remaining permanently in the UK (Marshall, 1991).

In the European context, refugees seeking asylum are nothing new. The USA is an abiding monument to asylum seekers from Europe. For hundreds of years, Jews and Gypsies have been harried across and out of Europe. The Second World War produced some sixty million refugees, including some twenty million Germans, and even now, in a world emerging from the Cold War, it is estimated that some fifteen million people are refugees. Within Europe, the collapse of Yugoslavia has produced an estimated two and a half million refugees, the majority of whom remain within the old borders of that state. By September 1992, about 250,000 had arrived in Germany, and some 30,000 in the UK (Rutter, 1991, pp 26 and 35; Rutter and Fischer, 1992). However, the actual number given formal refugee status in the UK is only about three thousand. Three years later, the numbers are almost certainly greater, for as the situation in the former Yugoslavia changes so rapidly, the only thing one can be reasonably certain about is that all these figures are probably a considerable underestimate of the actual number of refugees. People from Yugoslavia are not the sole source of European refugees. There is every likelihood of more refugees from other parts of Europe coming into schooling systems throughout the European Union during the next decade, as new nationalisms and xenophobic tendencies arise from the ashes of Soviet Communism.

Although prediction is difficult, it is still important, that as refugees and asylum seekers arrive in the major cities of the European Union, help is given to education systems to meet their children's needs more adequately. The next section of this chapter looks at this, using refugees in UK schools as an example of the sorts of issues that major city educational systems are currently facing across the European Union. The anglocentric example should not obscure the fact that refugees are a European Union-wide phenomenon and that there are certainly far more in Germany than in the UK.

8.3. The Education of Refugees in the UK

The growth of refugees internationally has a symbiotic relationship with current manifestations of nationalism, ethnic (including religious) chauvinism and concepts of the modern state. One consequence of this in the UK context is that refugees have seldom been welcomed, despite the English belief that they have always been welcoming to political refugees. This belief was fostered by some famous individual refugees from the nineteenth century like Marx and Mazzini. Poor Irish and Jewish refugees in the nineteenth century were rarely welcomed; in this century, Jews were denied entry in the 1930s. In relation to schooling, they seldom received much aid from the state, having to rely often on their own resources, frequently strongly supported by their religious groups.

The current position confirms the historical continuity. Asylum seekers continue to arrive in the UK, from other parts of Europe and the rest of the world. The most significant groups currently are refugees from the former Yugoslavia and from states in the Horn of Africa. This relates to political and media significance rather than to actual numbers. In the period since 1970, the numerically significant groups of refugees in the UK have been from Uganda, Cyprus, Vietnam, Iran, Sri Lanka, Somalia, former Yugoslavia and Kurds from Iran, Iraq and Turkey. The majority, some eighty per cent, stay in the London area, making them a significant presence in the capital's schools (Rutter, 1994). However, despite their numbers, their pattern of migration can result in the refugees leading quite isolated and economically marginal lives. Currently, in London for example, there is considerable concern for Somali women refugees, particularly over their marginality and the inability of the usual social agencies to assist them.

So how have London schools responded to refugee students? As outlined in the opening section of this chapter, the traditional assimilation, integration, cultural pluralism taxonomy of educational responses to diversity, implying some sort of linear progression is no longer tenable within the UK context. It is now clear that responses to diversity over the last thirty or so years in the schools of the UK show few clear trends. Xenophobia currently flourishes with its, at best, assimilationist views on education. Pluralism is mixed up with debates about subsidiarity, which, in the English context, seem to mean a plurality of national states rather than nations *within* a state. The English barely recognise Welsh and Scots claims to subsidiarity, and do little to support them in practice. All three groups would readily give such rights to Northern Ireland, to rid themselves of a political impasse to which they see no real solution.

The sudden arrival of numbers of refugee children, or, perhaps more accurately, the sudden public and educational attention being given to such children, seems to have triggered off responses that demonstrate the propensity in much of the education system to learn little from its own history. Thus many schools consider that the policies in place for other groups of ethnic minority students are perfectly suitable for the new refugee children. In other words, the issue is a technical one, based on deficit models of learning and assimilationist models of society. In this case, the students lack English: teach it to them and they can access the curriculum like any student. Of course, the acquisition of English is a crucial part in accessing the curriculum, but so also is sensitive understanding, and a range of educational strategies for dealing with other obstacles to learning that refugee children might bring with them or have imposed upon them by schools and the wider society.

However, it is difficult for education systems and teachers to understand the full range of obstacles that exist. Many relate to the traumatic experiences that led to asylum seeking, some involving death and torture. Others relate to the difficulties of surviving in the UK, in making sense of the bureaucratic systems that impinge on all aspects of refugees' life here. They often feel insecure and isolated and indeed they often are. Within this environment, school is potentially one of the few secure sites in their daily lives and teachers can be critically important adults. However, for teachers to deal effectively with such issues requires training. At a time of financial stringency, such training may well not seem a major priority area for schools, even those with significant numbers of refugee children. So well-intentioned *ad hoc* responses at an individual teacher or individual school level are more likely.

Despite this, many refugee students survive within the education system and many will even succeed. But at times this is achieved despite the system rather than because of it. Yet there is much that schools can do. There is some excellent school practice which the educational system as a whole can build upon. As mentioned earlier, the vast majority of refugee children in the UK attend schools in inner London. Inner city schools there nearly all have some refugee children, in some instances up to thirty per cent of the pupil population. The responses of schools fall into four main categories of activity: firstly, work relating to language development and acquisition; secondly, work encouraging schools, teachers and non-refugee pupils to gain a greater awareness of refugee issues; often this involves giving background information about new refugee groups; thirdly, assisting refugee children and their families with housing, employment, legal status and so on; fourthly, work that assists teachers and students to deal with trauma; in particular, this deals with assisting pupils and students who have been the victims or observers of torture.

Much of the work done under these categories is school-initiated and funded by teacher goodwill rather than by the education system. Early intercultural work in UK schools in the 1970s was done in a similar way before being taken up and properly funded by local education authorities (LEAs). The problem now is that the ability of the LEA to allocate extra resources into this field is very limited due to the winding down of their function and, in London at any rate, their chronic lack of resources. As in-service education and training money is increasingly delegated to schools, the danger is that the educational needs of refugees will be placed in competition with the educational needs of other disadvantaged groups in the school, to the long term detriment of all.

Despite these considerable difficulties, much good work is being done. Long and well-established school-based English as a second language programmes have readily adapted, technically, to the needs of refugee children. But these programmes vary in quality from school to school and whether refugee children and young people receive good or inadequate language support is a lottery. Meeting their first language needs has been far less successful, reflecting the lack of trained people, as well as the fact (highlighted in Chapter Nine) that this remains an undeveloped area of the UK school curriculum.

Information about the more recent refugee groups and their educational needs is slowly appearing (British Refugee Council 1991; Rutter, 1994). The Minority Rights Group and the Refugee Council have produced excellent general material for use in schools (and elsewhere) and inner London local education authorities have started to produce relevant materials, particularly background information on the more recently arrived groups. Recent work (Kasabova, 1991; Rutter and Fischer, 1992; Warner, 1991; Somali Relief Association 1991) shows that appropriate and valuable material is being produced, although whether teachers are aware of its existence is another matter. Moving the materials production process on to teaching about the factors that lead to asylum seeking is already a part of this process. However, pressures on teachers and schools due to the government's draconian programme of educational change slows down classroom implementation. A further area, teaching about persecution and the place of refugees within UK society, is still only at a rudimentary stage in most schools.

This last point links in with the third category of school response mentioned earlier, namely that teachers and schools are having to take on a general welfare role in relation to some of their refugee children. This is a role for which they have neither been trained nor resourced. Yet gaps in the official welfare net leave teachers often as the only mediators and negotiators with state bureaucracy.

The final issue, that of dealing with trauma, is complex. As Martenson (1992, p.ii) advocates, there is a need for 'training to prepare teachers and parents to better handle war traumatised children', and such training should be 'a long term commitment.' Although Martenson's report deals with the educational needs of children in Croatia and Slovenia, many of the comments made in the report would apply equally to refugee children who have sought safety in other European countries. The report goes on to discuss the traumas such children have faced: 'Only the trained psychologists with whom the mission met spoke of the need to come to terms with a perhaps more disturbing and intractable truth: withdrawn, angry, suspicious children as well as listless or vengeful parents' (Martenson, 1992, p.9). The likelihood of such care being provided at an adequate level remains slender in London, as it does in most other cities in Europe where refugee and asylum-seeking children are concentrated.

Yet experience in London schools suggests that teachers of refugees are likely to be dealing with such issues, often long after the refugee student has started at the school. Although many London teachers are experienced in dealing with a wide range of pastoral issues, including physical and sexual abuse of children, the experiences of some refugee children are extremely difficult to deal with. What is important to realise is that help in this area is needed by both the refugee children and the teachers most closely concerned with them, if the more extreme and unpleasant forms of experience are being dealt with.

The schools in London are doing valuable work but feel that they could and should do more. However, in the UK at least, official concern for the educational needs of asylum seekers remains a low priority. In many ways, this lack of concern reflects the more general inability of European Union states effectively to deal with the underlying issues that lead to asylum seeking in the first place. Whether more could be done about this more general issue relates to whether schools and universities *within* the European Union should in effect be 'more' European. The concerns surrounding this are the theme of the next chapter.

9.2. Regional, National and European Cultures: Beyond the Folklore Museum

Chapter Four considered the nature of the boundaries of Europe in political, economic and cultural terms. The theme of Europeanisation and the European Dimension in Education, espoused by the various bureaucracies of the Union, is based on an assumption of stable and readily recognisable boundaries to the continent. In fact these boundaries are far from clear, whether considered in political, economic or cultural terms. In political terms the boundaries of Europe might be identified with the boundaries of the Union itself. As the Union gains in size, self-confidence and internal coherence, this confusion is all too easily made. In terms of the European Union, Europe has expanded dramatically as three additional member states signed the Maastricht Treaty and acceded to membership on the first of January 1995. A queue of would-be members stretches across the Carpathians and the Bosphorous. Europe seems to be an expansive, even explosive, political-geographical entity. Less obviously, the day will come when states will wish to leave the European Union. This political and administrative identification will one day shrink even as it is now expanding. Like Foucault's view of epistemology, the European Union is an historical episode. There is and will be a Europe beyond the European Union in both geographical and historical terms.

In economic terms, the European Union is a major participant in world trade. Despite its huge internal production and market, the Union has no aspiration to limit its trade with the rest of the world, though it might attempt to control it through mechanisms such as GATT (General Agreement on Tariffs and Trade). It continues the pattern of international trade and, wherever possible, exploitation, on which the success of Europe's cities and states is based. In economic terms, Europe has no boundaries. Many non-European nations regret this now, as they have had cause to regret it in the past (Swift, (ed) 1994).

In political and economic terms, then, Europe does not have any clear boundaries. On the contrary, it is highly indeterminate. Whether tight cultural boundaries can ever be determined for Europe is, in a way, the theme of the remainder of this chapter.

Behind the creation of the European Union were cultural forces as well as, and at least as strong as, the political and economic. The states and cities which Europeans perceive to have played the most active part in the formation of their culture now all belong to the European Union. This would not have been the case without, say, Athens or Amsterdam. The theme of Europeanisation is itself a manifestation of the power of this cultural impulsion. Of course there is also a political reason for the European Union to spend such generous sums on this theme. The more the children and young people of Europe learn within a Europeanised curriculum the more they are likely to grow up to endorse European union and the political and bureaucratic institutions which support it.

The Europeanisation of the school and university curricula is an unparalleled political intervention on the culture of the continent. This attempt at the creation of a unitary cosmopolitan culture includes European science and knowledge within its delineation of curricular systems (Coulby, 1992; 1993) (see Chapter Seven). Europeanisation of the curriculum may be seen as a progressive and creative fusion, a harmonisation. As a powerful and deep-rooted cultural force, it may, however, have costs as well as benefits.

Europeanisation of the curriculum, for instance, might not further the European Union policy aspiration of widening as well as deepening the Union. If the Europeanised curricula stress the traditionalist and modernist accounts of European culture, then some countries on the periphery may be increasingly perceived as marginal or even hostile. If European knowledge and culture are perceived as being Christian in terms of Catholicism and Protestantism and democratic-capitalist, then how will the Europeanised curriculum present the cultures of Islamic and Orthodox countries and of those now emerging from totalitarian state-directed economies? Are the proponents of Europeanised culture and knowledge prepared to recognise the contributions of Prague, Moscow and Istanbul to its formation? Or of Cluj, Timosoara and Brasov? As was shown in Chapter Seven, in fact, the traditionalist and modernist versions of European culture perceive it as being closely geographically confined. The Europeanised curriculum may set in train cultural forces which limit the growth of the European Union at the same time as they encourage a strengthening and homogenisation within its boundaries.

In one sense Europeanisation of the school and university curricula flies in the face of fact. Neither Europe nor its cultures are unitary. There is not a common culture between the United Kingdom and Spain. To concentrate on the common culture between the two states may be to seek a lowest common denominator which takes away the richness of each. Indeed there is no common culture *within* the United Kingdom or Spain. The histories of the formation of the European states are a record of the attempt to impose unity on heterogeneity (Braudel, 1985a; 1985b; 1985c; 1989; 1990). The success of the unitary modernist endeavour is still very much in doubt in Catalonia, Brittany, Scotland and Lombardy. Can the Castilian curriculum adequately reflect the contribution of Barcelona? Let alone the conflicts between Castile and Catalonia?

Some exemplification, from languages and history, is offered in the next paragraphs to explain the links between curriculum, cultural formation and reformation and regional, national and continental identities. Whilst the two exemplars of languages and history are selected as important, so are other areas of the school curriculum, especially national language and literature teaching, religious education and science..

Already a firm plank in the Europeanisation of the school curriculum is the expansion of language teaching: more pupils should be able to learn more languages. This, it might be supposed, would lead towards more heterogeneity and away from unitary knowledge. But second language teaching in the Union is overwhelmingly the teaching of English. Even in those school systems, rapidly decreasing in number, where English is not the first foreign language, pupils and students opt with their purses during or after their school years by attending commercial English language classes. There are sound career reasons for this in the current economic order, reasons which are connected with financial history.

Where English is not the first foreign language or where second and third options are available to pupils and students, the languages studied tend to be those of the other large powers of the Union; French and German and, to a lesser extent, Spanish and Italian. There are reasons to be concerned about the status of the less powerful official languages of the Union; Greek, Dutch, Danish, Swedish, Finnish and Portuguese. Concern, that is, for their status within the Union: Portuguese remains a major world language and Greek has a huge international diaspora. This is even more true for those national minority languages which are spoken within or between the states of the Union, but which are not recognised as being among its official languages. Welsh is still taught in Wales and Catalan in Catalonia. But how much is Welsh taught in England or Catalan in Castile? None at all. And the idea of teaching Catalan to English pupils would be considered absurd.

Another popular theme for the European dimension in the curriculum is history (Hostermark Tarrou, 1993; Millat, 1993). The history of the formation, struggles and imperialism of the great European powers — Spain, Portugal, the Netherlands, France, the UK, Germany and Italy — form much of the history curriculum, even where it has been Europeanised. At issue here is both the content and approach of the school and university curriculum for history: the history of which country, or part of country, or countries? In what way are its international interactions to be considered? The history of which period? Will the history be merely political or will it include social, economic and cultural history? Is history to be known and told or to be uncertain and investigated? A more European history might look at the development of the religious and economic beliefs and institutions and at the social conditions of various groups in various epochs alongside the emergence of political systems. The Thirty Years War (Rogers, 1993) or the Industrial Revolution might be themes that open a more European understanding for students than the conquests of, say, Ferdinand and Isabella or of Napoleon.

But even so the history and achievement of the minority populations of Europe and of the less dominant regions would remain hidden. Indeed the very process whereby they had become minority and hidden — the long painful histories of Brittany and the Vendee or of the Mezzogiorno — would be concealed. Before England embarked on world conquest it dominated first Wales, Scotland and Ireland. The domination of Scotland culminated at Culloden and led to the pacification (and depopulation) of the Highlands and Islands. At the very time that this was happening, intellectuals in the Lowlands of Scotland, especially in Edinburgh, were playing a major part in the emerging Enlightenment. Should the European theme in history make some explanation of these events available to pupils in Inverness? in London? in Grenada? If such explanations are not made available then the histories and even the major achievements — the Scottish Enlightenment, the Cordoba Caliphate — of minority populations and less politically and economically favoured regions will become invisible; folklore museums for uncomprehending and bored tourists from the central European metropolis.

These cannot be dismissed as small scale or marginal issues: a far from comprehensive list of those regions whose population might espouse a radically different version of history from that maintained by their states would include Andalusia, Catalonia, the Basque country, Brittany, Languedoc, Corsica, Friesland, the Alto Adige, the Mezzogiorno, Sicily, Macedonia, Northern Ireland, Wales and Scotland.

In the case of languages, some of the actual states of the Union as well as its multitude of regions find themselves excluded from the Europeanisation of the curriculum. In the case of history, Europeanisation might serve further to bury the history of those groups of people still struggling to resist the imposition of centralising states. This chapter is not simply arguing that Europeanisation and the European dimension in the curriculum are a Bad Thing. Would that the issue were so simple. What it is seeking to analyse is a conflict between, on the one hand, the centripetal force of Europeanisation pulling culture and knowledge towards the metropolitan centre and, on the other, the centrifugal forces of local, regional and even national identities pulling outwards towards the preservation and reformulation of heterogeneity.

9.3. International Migration and European Culture: Empires and Error

This conflict model, with its familiar cultural cartography of centre and periphery, would be readily comprehensible, but unfortunately it is not the whole story. This simple model is complicated by historical patterns of migration in and between the countries of the European Union and into the Union from outside. The demographic patterns of these migrations are well described elsewhere (Noin and Woods, (eds) 1993). From the point of view of European culture, these patterns of migration add a further layer of complexity to the languages and knowledge systems held by the people of the European Union. (For recent descriptions of the development of intercultural education within the states of Europe see Broadbent, 1994 (the UK); Campani, 1994 (Italy); Liauzu, 1994 (France); Fase, 1994 (the Netherlands); Garcia-Castano, and Moyano, 1993 (Spain); Lammers, 1993 (Denmark); Marcou, 1993 (Greece); Martiniello, and Manco, 1993 (French speaking Belgium); Reich, 1994 (Germany); Szabio, 1993 (Hungary); Trindade, and Medes, 1993 (Portugal); Szaday, 1994 (Switzerland); Grant, 1994 (Scotland)). The main thrust of this section of the argument concerns those populations from Anatolia, Asia, Africa and Latin and Caribbean America who have settled in the cities of the European Union in the period of economic expansion which followed 1945. However, the argument could also be extended to the inter-European migration patterns especially of people from the South and the East to the cities of the North or indeed, more simply, from all countries of Europe into the cities of the Western part of Germany: 'Between 1988 and 1992 about 4.2 million persons entered the territory of the FRG' (Gieseck et al, 1994 p. 15). In addition the itinerant population of gypsies and travellers provides member states with an unrecognised and misunderstood culture and with unresolved educational difficulties (Council of Europe 1983; 1986; 1987; 1989; 1990; 1991; 1992a; 1992b; 1992c). Furthermore, German speaking people 'returning' to the cities of the West from East Prussia or Transylvania bring with them distinct traditions and cultural patterns almost as fragile in Cologne as in present day Romania and Poland.

The wider interpretation of the concept of culture must be kept in mind. The populations from Africa and Asia which have become resident in the cities of the European Union bring with them not quaint, folkloric habits of costume and gastronomically adventurous cuisines and dietary practices. The cultures they represent include languages of major international importance such as Chinese, Hindi or Bengali, and others much more limited and fragile; in many cases the groups speak more than one language or regional dialect. Their religions too, are often representative of huge international faith communities such as Muslims, Hindus or Sikhs. Others continue the less known religious systems of smaller groups. The cultures associated with these languages and religions include not only literature, art and music but also philosophy, science, technology, medicine and law (Van Boven, 1993; Witteck et al 1993).

The impact of these populations on the cultural and educational map of the European Union is profound. Their presence, especially in the large cities of the Union, is a further exposure of the absurdity of a unitary national or pan-European culture. There are over two hundred languages spoken by children in the schools of London. Islam is a major religious and communal force in Frankfurt and Berlin. These populations have often migrated to the metropolitan centres of the previously colonising (politically and/or economically) power: Surinamese and Moluccans to Amsterdam, Magrhebians to Paris and Marseilles, West Indians and people from the subcontinent of India to London and Birmingham, Turks to Stuttgart and Munich, Chilean refugees to Madrid and now Ethiopians and Magrhebians to Naples and Milan. Consequently they have views concerning European imperialism and economic colonialism which are often in stark contrast with that of other constituents of the urban population or of state-controlled school and university systems.

In terms of languages, then, the school curriculum is faced with a set of political difficulties. It seems uncontestable that all children should learn the language of the state in which they live. But some countries of the Union and some large cities have more than one official language. Should Arabic-speaking children in Brussels learn French or Flemish or both? Should Bangladeshi-speaking young people in Cardiff learn Welsh or English or both? The nature of the languages supported also needs to be considered. Should the school systems of the Union maintain the heritage languages of the children and young people in the schools and universities? This is administratively possible, if politically unpopular, in areas of high concentration such as with Arabic-speaking people in Lyons or Bangladeshi-speakers in the Tower Hamlets area of London. In areas where there is a high diversity of heritage languages, and some primary schools in London have over forty languages spoken by their children, the very administration of heritage language development presents almost insuperable difficulties to reluctant local and national education authorities.

Languages present curriculum planners with a political minefield. This paragraph uses the example of London only because it is one of the most complex. Parallel issues exist in all the countries of the Union. When Sylheti-speaking Londoners are taught a language at school why should this be French or German as against Bengali itself? If they are not able to achieve accredited examination success in their own language then their academic and commercial potential is surely being as under-utilised as their culture is being unrecognised. Furthermore, when English speaking pupils from an area of London with a high percentage of Sylheti speakers choose a language why should this not be Sylheti rather than French or German?

Sylheti is the more widely-spoken language internationally of the three and furthermore it is likely to allow the pupils to communicate with their urban neighbours on a daily basis rather than with other Europeans on an occasional holiday. The theme of Europeanisation would insist that the English speaking pupils (above all!) should learn other languages of the Union but this is again to neglect and negate the actual cultural and linguistic diversity of London. The linguistic, cultural and commercial strength of London, like so many cities of the Union, lies in its diversity. Any attempt to homogenise it in the interests of Europeanisation will only lead to the destruction of this diversity and the erosion of this strength.

The example of history need not be so anglocentric. The point is well made by Braudel:

> Similarly, the present-day territory of France ... is not the only standard of measurement we need refer to. Within it are sub-measurements: regions, provinces, *pays*, which long maintained, and which still do maintain a significant degree of autonomy; while beyond it there is Europe and beyond Europe the world. ... one might go on to say 'there is no such thing as European history, there is world history' ... (Braudel 1989 p 20).

The chronicle of centralisation and domination within the states which now make up the Union is not confined to the peoples within their boundaries, however these are defined. The Empires of Portugal, Spain, Holland, England and France have had a profound influence on the economies, politics and cultures of huge areas of the world. Belgium, Germany and Italy played a smaller but not insignificant part in these transformations. Many of the major imperialistic powers of the last millennium are now member states of the Union. Any history of these states individually or collectively must either be world history or be error. Yet seen from a world perspective this is largely a history of conquest, subjugation, slavery, genocide and exploitation, which hardly reflects creditably on the countries concerned. This perspective is frequently that of those urban migrant groups whose countries have witnessed the record of European imperialism from the receiving end. The history curricula of the European states are in some cases attempting to address these issues and in many others to avoid them.

Ignoring or disguising these issues fails to reflect the heterogeneity of the culture of present day Europe. But this heterogeneity is itself only new in degree rather than in kind. Heterogeneity has been a feature of the large powerful cities of the continent at least since the Roman Republic. The mighty cities of Europe's emergence — Venice, Genoa, Antwerp, Amsterdam, London — bear witness to an openness to the outside world. Certainly this openness is most obviously seen in terms of trade and subsequent conquest, but it is also there in a receptivity to new ideas, products and practices (Braudel, 1985a; 1985b; 1985c). Furthermore, a cultural diversity of population characterised these powerful cities in the past just as it does today.

This openness may be demonstrated in cultural and knowledge terms. A detailed analysis of Islamic and Byzantine influences on the Renaissance is hardly needed here. The Moorish-Norman buildings of Naples and Sicily make the point as strongly as the Byzantine basilica of St Mark's. But the influences go beyond art and architecture into technical, financial and mercantile processes, exegesis of Greek and Roman texts, science and mathematics. Indeed mathematics, so often presented as one of the highest planes of European achievement, is at least as much the product of Asian and African skill (Joseph, 1992). Indeed, Europe's cultural strength may be seen to reside in its periods of openness to its own heterogeneity rather than in any attempts at closure or imposed unity. The record of cultural closure is one of Europe's bloodiest, through crusades, inquisitions and the slave trade to the Holocaust. The influence of migrating groups within Europe and from beyond is not a new phenomenon, but over a long period one of the most important influences on the formation of European knowledge and culture.

In curricular terms, the issue is the extent to which the dimensions and nature of this diversity can be reflected in the school and university curriculum, and the extent to which this theme is intrinsically opposed to or in harmony with the theme of Europeanisation. Is Europeanisation, with its inevitable tendencies towards centralisation and homogenisation, opposed to postmodernist conceptions of historical knowledge? Perhaps it is too early to answer this question affirmatively. A more postmodernist approach to history might stress the uncertainty of all evidence, the arbitrariness of the selection of epoch and geographical area, the relativity and transitoriness of political achievement, the political and nationalistic motivation behind much European historiography, the history of non-dominant groups and regions, women's history, oral history, the records of resistance to European colonisation and exploitation. Whether the incorporation of the European dimension will encourage this approach remains to be seen but the past record does not give too many grounds for optimism.

9.4. Nationalist Knowledge

This chapter has presented some of the conflicts between the hetero-geneous knowledge and culture current in the European Union and the well-meant process of Europeanisation. In order to sharpen the contrast it has deliberately overlooked the still dominant curricular influence in many of the member states, namely central national governments. In some countries of the Union, such as Greece, curricular prescription continues even to the extent of the designation of textbooks. In other countries, such as France, a central system is slowly relaxing its tight grip (McLean, 1990). In England and Wales a National Curriculum is being remarkably unsuccessfully enforced on reluctant teachers, schools and localities (Bash and Coulby, 1989; Coulby and Bash, 1991).

These national curricular systems, of which that in England and Wales is a prime and retrograde example, are impervious to either regional influence or multicultural knowledge systems on the one hand or to Europeanisation on the other. They are typified by at least the following characteristics: a concentration on the purity of the national language; an emphasis on national literature; science and technology stressed as adjuncts to capitalist enterprise; a revisionist concentration on national history, ideologically codified to present a chronicle of the heroic progress of a mainly white and male civilisation; religion presented in partial and often compulsory denominational codes. National and nationalist curricular systems tend to employ the rhetoric of heritage. The heritage is exclusive to the people who can claim their ancestry back into a proud chauvinistic past. Regional and migrant groups are the victims of this curriculum just as in the past they were the victims of the events and movements now jingoistically reinterpreted: 'the birth of the nation', 'the national language' etc. The state curricula purvey cultural imperialism in the countries of the

European Union as much as Europe's literatures, films, pop-music, commodity fetishism and higher education penetrate cultural domination beyond the boundaries of the continent.

Such a curriculum is touchingly untroubled by the difficulties of introducing Europeanisation. Against the National Curriculum of England and Wales or the language obsessions of the current French government, the European theme would be a breath of fresh air. At least through Europeanisation some sense of a wider international community, a richer and less certain history, a more heterogeneous and interactive culture may be made available.

Depending on the existing cultural practices in a state, region or institution, then, the European dimension may be a threat or a source of liberation. It is a threat to the heterogeneous vitality of the continent's culture but it could offer a source of liberation from dominant nationalistic knowledge systems. Whether it is a threat or a source of liberation will differ as it affects each state, region or city. It will also depend on how the next tranche of Europeanisation is constructed. Finally, it will depend on wider political events, not least the progress towards widening and deepening the Union. Whether the emergent postmodernist version of knowledge can tangibly influence school and university curricula without these political constraints remains doubtful.

Chapter Ten

POSTMODERNITY AND EDUCATIONAL POLICY

It is the traditional responsibility of all who write on education to have at least half an answer to the teachers' perennial question as to what is to be done on Monday morning. An educational text with little purchase on school and university practice has dubious value. This is not arguing for an exclusively 'tips for teachers' approach, although books of that sort clearly have their place and value. It is, however, to assert that the debates about modernity, postmodernity and late modernity that form the focus of this book have clear implications for institutional practice at all levels in the education system, from the national government to the individual classroom. Previous chapters have attempted to indicate how such a discussion can affect educational practice. This final chapter is also concerned with this key question, locating the discussion in a wide range of educational debates, in order to assert the necessity for many discourses if an effective education is to be provided for all the children and young people in schools and colleges throughout Europe.

This book grew out of earlier attempts to explain some of the issues facing education in the cities of England towards the end of the twentieth century. Despite a decade of Government-inspired changes in the administration and structure of education, we did not think the issues of providing a complete and successful education for all young people were being tackled any more efficiently than at any other time in the recent educational past. The teachers in urban schools are, in the main, well trained and also attend frequent in-service education sessions. Many of them are dedicated to what they do, despite frequent denigration from certain politicians and sections of the press. Also, in the main, the parents want their children to be happy and successful at school. Many of the follies introduced in the 1988 Education Act have gone, although many remain to make life more difficult for schools and those who work in them. However, some of the 1988 changes, such as delegated budgets, have brought benefit to schools; similarly the polytechnics and colleges have undoubtedly benefited from their freedom from local control, so the judgement on that extraordinary piece of politically-motivated legislation seems remarkably uneven.

So why do certain groups of children not succeed as well as they might? Part of the difficulty of understanding such issues is the narrowness of focus. City schools cannot be understood in isolation. They need to be examined within the English national context where they are located. Furthermore, English schools need to be placed in their UK, their European Union and their international context. Indeed, no state system of education can succeed in giving full educational rights to all children if these wider contexts are ignored. This has meant that this book has concentrated on the European Union as well as the national context to explain what is and is not happening in schools in England as well as in Europe more generally. Furthermore, how minority students, however defined, are educated seemed critical to this concern for educational success. To gain any grasp on these issues, the complexities had to be investigated, hence the concern in this book with debates about the nature and status of modernity. As Stuart Hall and his colleagues put it, we need to understand, among other things,

> the meaning and implications of the collapse of communism in Russia and Eastern Europe; shifts in the dynamics and organisation of the global capitalist economic order; the changing forms of contemporary culture and identity formation; the growing interconnectedness between states and societies; and challenges to that quintessentially modern political institution, the nation-state. (Hall et al, 1992, p.1).

This book has attempted part of that task of understanding in relation to education. It has concentrated on those factors internal to the education system, or perhaps more accurately, those factors which can be changed or influenced by the education system. This explains the book's preoccupation with issues relating to school and university knowledge. This preoccupation does not mean that these areas are the only ones that help explain educational success or failure. There are clearly a whole range of issues relating to school organisation, didactics and pedagogy which are crucial and about which there is still too little known. However, what has been examined in the book do impinge on all these aspects. One reason for this is that the knowledge systems that those working in education bring to the task are seldom analysed, with many believing that a consensus exists on such matters.

In English educational politics, there was an illusion of consensus about the shape of state education from the mid 1940s until the late 1970s. Perhaps its clearest professional exposition was in the work and the pronouncements of HMI, supported by influential headteachers, educational administrators and academics. Such a consensus, even an illusory consensus, was not typical of educational politics in Europe more generally. In many of the states of Eastern Europe Soviet educational theory and practice had been imposed, with criticism and conflict being possible only in the most circumspect of ways. In many countries in Western Europe such as France, church/state conflicts still continued. In addition to the secular/religious divisions, other states, such as Italy and Spain, had left/right divides over educational practice. More, in many countries of Europe, access to higher education remains one of the most fiercely fought political issues. This has meant that dramatic and contested changes in educational practice are as much the norm within Europe as a peacefully evolving consensus.

However, despite their frequent fierceness, most of these debates took place within the framework set by the Enlightenment project discussed in earlier chapters of this book. Curiously enough, it was conservative politicians in the USA and the UK who first started to challenge the ground rules of this debate. This dismissal of the basic 'rules of the game' was clearly expressed by the UK Conservative politician (and later, Secretary of State for Education) Sir Keith Joseph, who asserted:

> The blind, unplanned, uncoordinated wisdom of the market....is overwhelmingly superior to the well researched, rational, systematic, well meaning, co-operative, science based, forward looking, statistically respectable plans of governments.... (Quoted in Jones, K., 1989, p.46).

Although this may merely seem a restatement of the antiquated non-interventionist theories of the eighteenth century French physiocrats

(Sharma, 1989), it is in fact a very definite rejection of much of the modern agenda. It could indeed be seen as an archetypical postmodern assertion.

The dramatic changes in education brought about by the proponents of these and similar views when they acquired political power were most apparent in the English speaking world, most noticeably in certain states in Australia and the United States and in England and Wales. As attempts to solve some of the deep structural problems in their respective societies, it is perhaps too early to judge their effectiveness, although the initial impressions are far from favourable. In educational terms, the introduction of the market into the education system has done little for minorities, who have little market power, economic, political or educational. As in the previous experiment in selection, a few working class and minority students may get on the ladder, legitimising the whole experiment in the eyes of many of the changes' supporters. The danger is that this Anglo-Saxon model may be uncritically imported by other countries, especially those in Eastern Europe currently undergoing radical restructuring. As was made clear in Chapter Eight, the educational structural implications of postmodern theory may be for fractured, unequal and competing institutions at all phases.

As the difficulties in the modern educational agenda become more clear and as political solutions, from both the left and the right have been judged to be unsuccessful, two strands of educational response have become more apparent, one which may be characterised as the 'Canute Approach' the other as the 'Toolmaker Approach'. Both are attempts to put the derailed Enlightenment project back on its tracks and both make a ready appeal to those teachers who demand of educational theory an immediate response to their daily exigencies.

To take the more simplistic one first. The Canute Approach was put forward as a major policy basis by the UK Prime Minister, John Major in the early 1990s. Characterised by the slogan 'Back to Basics', it faced the dilemmas of the late modern social and educational agenda by commanding them to go away with a Canute-like gesture. In speeches and interviews, he evoked a vision of England and English life as a revival of as a 1930s suburban life-style of bliss and order. That this was a myth and potentially a dangerous one had been exposed by Lewis Mumford who argued that the

> suburb served as an asylum for the preservation of illusion. Here
> domesticity could flourish, forgetful of the exploitation on which so

much of it was based. Here individuality could prosper, oblivious of the pervasive regimentation beyond. This was not merely a child centred environment, it was based on a childish view of the world....(Mumford, 1961, p.563.)

If back to basics is indeed, 'a childish view of the world', it retains significant educational power. Its educational touchstones in the UK include spelling tests, an attack on real books as an aid to reading, formal teaching methods, school uniform, streaming, selection and, if European law would only allow it, corporal punishment. These beliefs and practices were also the basis of the UK's mass education system in the nineteenth and first half of the twentieth century.

But the complexities of the modern world require a forward-looking reappraisal of the content and methodologies of education. There needs to be an increasing awareness that there is no longer a one best system and that a plurality of approach is probably required. How can the insights of postmodernity be made relevant to the structuring of educational systems? It is not surprising that such a perspective, holding out the potential for the maintenance and increase of inequality, was first espoused by the radical right. For the left, with its traditional commitment to centralising tendencies, such moves to greater pluralism of provision seemed anti-egalitarian. Thus, for the left, provision such as single sex schools, religious schools or self-selecting all-black schools are not automatically welcomed. There is as yet no clear statement of the educational means by which diversity can be preserved without sacrificing the principle of equality.

The Canute approach, although politically powerful, does little to improve the quality of schooling for many of the children and young people who are the main concern of this book. At this point, enter the toolmakers. Generally progressive in intent, the Toolmaker approach has been a powerful influence on social policy in general and on education in particular. The key element in this approach is that education's failures are mainly failures in articulation; that more effective articulation of the structures leads to greater educational success for groups previously seen as failing in the system.

There have been at least three important experiments in this area in the UK: the Community Development Projects (CDP) and the Educational Priority Area Projects (EPA) of the late 1960s and the School Effectiveness movement that dominates much progressive educational discourse at present. The CDP experience is unduly neglected today as the questions that the projects raised remain largely unanswered. Set up in 1969, they were predicated on the view that disadvantaged groups did not make full benefit of systems set up to help them. This maintained the disadvantage. Greater take up, although costly in the short term would eventually lead to less disadvantage and thus, in the long term, save money. John Bennington, the leader of the Coventry CDP summed up the reasons for the failure of such projects in the following terms:

> The early formulations of the CDP experiment implied a consensus model of social change. This is based on the assumption that social problems are 'malfunctions' which can be cured by adjustments and rearrangements within the existing operating systems. The problems are defined mainly in terms of failures of co-ordination and communication, and the focus of change is thus on management and administration and the non-participant... Observation and experience in the project areas has led many CDP teams to reject this initial prescription in favour of a pluralist model of social change... The problems are defined mainly in terms of failures of participation and representation of certain interests in the political process, and the focus of change is thus on politicians, policy makers and the disenfranchised. (Bennington, 1975, p.186).

Similar conclusions came from the EPA schemes. Schools were given extra resources which were firstly, inadequate to the scale of the task and secondly, badly targeted (Barnes and Lucas, 1977). Technocratic intervention, albeit at an underfunded level, made little difference to the success of pupils or the lives of their parents.

Despite these failures, the toolmakers persisted. In many ways, they were right so to do. Starting in the USA in the 1970s, the school effectiveness movement gained considerable credit for detailed examinations of articulatory practice in American schools. A major manifestation in the UK was *Fifteen Thousand Hours* (Rutter et al, 1979). It appeared to demonstrate that schools could make a difference and that the factors accounting for such difference could be identified. It made these claims without any significant examination of curriculum content. This is symptomatic of one of the weaknesses of the Toolmaker approach. Its proponents believe that effective tools, if used correctly, will improve key elements in an educational institution's administrative and pedagogic practice. Whist this is valuable and education systems have benefited from the insights provided, it is only a small part of the picture. What is effectively taught and learned by using these tools is often completely neglected.

This book asserts that *what* educational task is done with these tools is both a prerequisite to their work and indeed, a more important issue. Thus, what is to be taught has to come before how it is to be taught. It is these prior questions that need re-examination in the light of our greater understanding of the complexities, ambiguities and contradictions of modern life. Furthermore, the nature of minorities, how they are defined within the state and within the European Union as a whole are basic factors that have to be clarified by and/or for teachers if they are effectively to teach the children for whom they have responsibility. Similarly the ways in which schools and universities reflect Europe's contribution to civilisation needs fundamental re-examination. The epistemological and curricular issues that have been raised in earlier chapters are inseparable from this definition and are necessarily anterior to any questions of educational effectiveness. To speak of a school or university which successfully teaches xenophobic science or history as effective is nonsense.

Acceptance of fracture and ambivalence and working out an appropriate educational agenda to prepare young people for an uncertain future is a difficult and challenging task. Key sites in the elaboration of this agenda are the colleges and universities that prepare people to teach. Far from concentrating on toolmaker competencies, teacher education should encourage intending teachers to examine more closely the nature of the knowledge which they wish to teach to the next generation. What teachers and lecturers consider to be knowledge will shape the activities and extent of the European Union. What they consider to be knowledge will play a part in determining the future harmony or discord of Europe. If xenophobia is to be reduced — as this book is completed a huge Russian army is fighting its way into Grozny — school and university knowledge needs to be transformed.

Bibliography

Appadurai, A. (1990) 'Disjuncture and Difference in the Global Cultural Economy' in Featherstone, M. (ed) (1990) *Global Culture: Nationalism, Globalisation and Modernity. A Theory, Culture and Society Special Issue.* London: Sage.

Archer, M. (1984) *Social Origins of Educational Systems.* London: Sage.

Aronowitz, S. and Giroux, H. (1991) *Postmodern Education: Politics, Culture and Social Criticism.* London: University of Minnesota Press.

Arora, R. and Duncan, C. (eds) (1986) *Multicultural Education: Towards Good Practice.* London: Routledge and Kegan Paul.

Balace, F. (1991) 'Russian nationalism from Tsarist imperialism to the present day' Paper presented to the *European Seminar on the Nationalities Question,* Beneux, Belgium, April 1991.

Baldwin, J. (1961) *Nobody Knows My Name.* New York: Dial Press.

Barber, T. (1994) 'Minorities emerge from the darkness' *The Independent,* 26 September 1994, p.8.

Barnes, J. and Lucas H. (1977) 'Positive Discrimination in Education, Individual Groups and Institutions' in Raggatt, P. and Evans, M. (eds) (1977) *The Political Context.* London: Ward Lock.

Bash, L. et al. (1985) *Urban Schooling: Theory and Practice.* London: Cassell.

Bash, L. and Coulby, D. (1989) *The Education Reform Act: Competition and Control.* London: Cassell.

Batelaan, P. (1983) *The Practice of Intercultural Education.* London: CRE

Batsleer, P. et al. (1985) *Rewriting English.* London: Methuen.

Bauman, Z. (1993) *Intimations of Postmodernity.* London: Routledge.

Bennington, J. (1975) 'The flaw in the pluralist heaven' in Lees, R and Smith, G. (eds) (1975) *Action Research in Community Development.* London: Routledge and Kegan Paul.

Bernal, M. (1987) *Black Athena: The Afroasiatic Roots of Classical Civilisation. Volume 1. The Fabrication of Ancient Greece 1785-1985.* London: Vintage.

Bernal, M. (1991) *Black Athena: The Afroasiatic Roots of Classical Civilisation. Volume II. The Archaeological and Documentary Evidence*. London: Free Association Press.

Bhabha, H. (1990) 'DissemiNation: time, narrative, and the margins of the modern nation' in Bhabha, H. (ed) (1990) *Nation and Narration*. London: Routledge.

Braudel, F. (1985a) *Civilisation and Capitalism 15th to 18th Century. Vol. 1. The Structures of Every day Life*. London: Collins.

Braudel, F. (1985b) *Civilisation and Capitalism 15th to 18th Century. Vol. 2.The Wheels of Commerce*. London: Collins.

Braudel, F. (1985c) *Civilisation and Capitalism 15th to 18th Century. Vol. 3. The Perspective of the World*. London: Collins.

Braudel, F. (1989) *The Identity of France: Volume 1. History and Environment*. London: Fontana.

Braudel, F. (1990) *The Identity of France: Volume 2. People and Production*. London: Fontana.

Brazier, C. (1994) 'Winds of Change'. *New Internationalist*, No. 262, pp.4-7.

Bredvold, L. (1956) *The Intellectual Milieu of John Dryden: Studies in some Aspects of Seventeenth-Century Thought*. Ann Arbor: University of Michigan Press.

Breuilly, J. (1985) *Nationalism and the State*. Manchester; Manchester University Press.

Bridge, A. (1993) 'Romanians vent old hatreds against Gypsies.' *The Independent*, 19 October 1993, p.13.

British Refugee Council [BRC] (1991) *Refugees in the Classroom*. London: British Refugee Council.

British Refugee Council (1993) *Who is a Refugee?* London: Refugee Council.

Broadbent, J. (1994) 'Education for a Multicultural Society in the United Kingdom'. *European Journal of Intercultural Studies*. 4, 3, pp 3-13.

Burchfield, R. (ed) (1972) *Supplement to the Oxford English Dictionary*. Vol. 1. Oxford: OUP.

Cameron, J. et al. (General eds) (1984) *International Handbook of Education Systems*. [3 volumes.] Chichester: John Wiley and Sons.

Campbell, B. and Lack, E. (eds) (1985) *A Dictionary of Birds*. Calton: T. and A.D. Poyser.

Cameron, D. (1985) *Feminism and Linguistic Theory*. New York: St. Martin's Press.

Campani, G. (1994) 'Intercultural Education in Italy'. *European Journal of Intercultural Studies*, 4, 3, pp 44-53.

CARF. (Campaign Against Racism and Fascism) (1994) *Deadly Europe*. London: CARF.

Carlsen, J. and Borga, O. (1993) *The Danish Folkehojskole*. Copenhagen: Royal Danish Ministry of Foreign Affairs.

Carter, B. (1993) 'Losing the Common Touch: a Postmodern Politics of the Curriculum?', *Curriculum Studies*, 1, 1, pp 149-156.

Castells, M. (1989) *The Informational City: Information Technology, Economic Restructuring and the Urban-Regional Process*. Oxford: Blackwell.

Cavafy, C. (1961) *The Complete Poems* [trans. Dalven, R.] London: The Hogarth Press.

Chant, C. (1991) 'Science in Orthodox Europe' in Goodman, D. and Russell, C. (eds) (1991) *The Rise of Scientific Europe 1500-1800*. London: Hodder and Stoughton..

Cole, M. (ed) (1989) *Education for Equality*. London: Routledge and Kegan Paul.

Coulby, D. (1991) 'The National Curriculum' in Coulby, D. and Bash, L. (1981) *Contradiction and Conflict: The 1988 Education Act in Action*. London: Cassell.

Coulby, D. (1992) 'Urban Civic Culture and Education' in Coulby, D. and Jones, C. (eds) (1992) *The 1992 World Yearbook of Education: Education and Urbanisation*. London: Kogan Page.

Coulby, D. (1993) 'Cultural and Epistemological Relativism and European Curricula'. *European Journal of Intercultural Studies*, 3, 2/3, pp 7-18.

Coulby, D. and Bash, L. (1991) *Contradiction and Conflict: The 1988 Education Act in Action*. London: Cassell.

Coulby, D. and Jones, C. (1989) 'Urban Education and Comparative Education: Some Possibilities' in McLean, M.(ed) (1989) *Education in Cities: International Perspectives*. London: British Comparative and International Education Society.

Coulby, D. and Jones, C. (eds) (1992) *The World Yearbook of Education 1992: Urban Education*. London: Kogan Page.

Coulby, D. and Ward, S. (eds) (1990) *The Primary Core National Curriculum: Education Policy into Practice*. London: Cassell.

Coulson, J. et al. (1980) *The Oxford Illustrated Dictionary Oxford:* O.U.P.

Council of Europe (1983) *Migrant Culture in a Changing Society: Multicultural Europe by the Year 2000*. Strasbourg: Council of Europe.

Council of Europe (1986) *Training Teachers in Intercultural Education?* Strasbourg: Council of Europe.

Council of Europe (1987) *The Education and Cultural Development of Migrants. Abstract of the Final Report of the Project Group.* Strasbourg: Council of Europe.

Council of Europe (1989) *Gypsy Children in Schools: Training for Teachers and other Personnel.* Strasbourg: Council of Europe.

Council of Europe (1990) *Final Educational Evaluation of the Programme of Experiments in Intercultural Education from 1986 to 1991.* Strasbourg: Council of Europe.

Council of Europe (1991) *Europe 1990-2000: Multiculturalism in the City. The Integration of Immigrants.* Strasbourg: Council of Europe.

Council of Europe (1992a) *Towards Intercultural Education — Training for Teachers of Gypsy Pupils.* Strasbourg: Council of Europe.

Council of Europe (1992b) *School Provision for Gypsy and Traveller Children: Distance Learning and Pedagogical Follow-Up.* Strasbourg: Council of Europe.

Council of Europe (1992c) *Schooling for Gypsies' and Travellers' Children — Evaluating Innovation.* Council of Europe: Strasbourg.

Cramp, S. et al. (1977 — 1994) *Handbook of the Birds of Europe, the Middle East and North Africa: The Birds of the Western Palaearctic.* Oxford: OUP.

Cronin, V. (1992a) *The Florentine Renaissance.* London: Pimlico.

Cronin, V. (1992b) *The Flowering of the Renaissance.* London: Pimlico.

Crystal, D. (1990) *The Cambridge Encyclopaedia.* Cambridge: C.U.P.

Davies, J. (1993) *History of Wales.* London: Alan Lane.

Dear, M and Scott, M. (eds) (1981) *Urbanisation and Urban Planning in Capitalist Society.* London: Methuen.

Dearing, R. (1993a) *The National Curriculum and its Assessment: Interim Report.* York/London: National Curriculum Council/Schools Examination and Assessment Council.

Dearing, R. (1993b) *The National Curriculum and its Assessment: Final Report.* London: Schools Curriculum and Assessment Authority.

Derrida, J. (1981) *Positions* (Translated Bass, A,) Chicago: University of Chicago Press.

DES. (Department of Education and Science) (1980) *Report by H.M. Inspectors on Educational Provision by the Inner London education Authority, Summer 1980.* London: DES.

DES (1985) *Education For All.* [The Swann Report.] London: HMSO.

DFE. (Department For Education.) (1993a) *Interim Report on the National Curriculum and its Assessment: The Government's Response*. London: DFE.

DFE. (Department For Education) (1993b) *Final Report on the National Curriculum and its Assessment: The Government's Response*. London: DFE.

DFE. (Department for Education) (1994) *National Curriculum Orders for England* (1994). (Second galley proofs without acknowledgement of publication.)

Delrot, J. (1992) *The Nationalities Question — From Versailles to the Present Day*. Strasbourg: Council of Europe.

Donne, J. (1935) *The Poems of John Donne*. Edited by H. Grierson. Oxford: OUP.

Dorn, M. (1993) ' 'We are discussing right wing extremism.' Education materials' in *European Journal of Intercultural Studies*. 4, 1.

Doyle, W. (1989) *The Oxford History of the French Revolution*. Oxford: OUP.

Dunant, S. (Ed.). (1994). *The War of the Words: the Political Correctness Debate*. London: Virago.

EC. (1992) *Treaty on European Union* [Maastricht Treaty] Brussels: EC.

Edwards, J. (1985) *Language, Society and Identity*. Oxford; Blackwell.

Eliot, T.S. (1955) *Selected Prose*. Harmondsworth: Penguin.

European Union (1994) 'Common Position (EC) no 33/94 ... with a view to adopting European Parliament and Council Decision 94/../EC of .. establishing the Community action programme 'Socrates' in *Official Journal of the European Communities* (C 244), Volume 37, pp.51-70.

Evans, B. and Waites B. (1981) *IQ. and Mental Testing*. London: Macmillan.

Fainstein, S.S. et al. (1992) *Divided Cities: New York and London in the Contemporary World*. Oxford: Blackwell.

Fainstein, S. S. (1994) *The City Builders: Property, Politics and Planning in London and New York*. Oxford: Blackwell.

Fase, W. (1993) 'Intercultural Education: the Dutch Way' in *European Journal of Intercultural Studies*, 4, 2, pp 49-58.

Featherstone, M. (ed) (1990) *Global Culture: Nationalism, Globalisation and Modernity. A Theory, Culture and Society Special Issue*. London: Sage.

Feyerabend, P. (1978a) *Against Method*. London: Verso.

Feyerabend, P. (1978) *Science in a Free Society*. London: Verso.

Fishman, J. (1975) *Language and Nationalism*. Roweley, Massachusetts; Newbury House.

Foucault, M. (1967) *Madness and Civilisation: A History of Insanity in the Age of Reason*. London: Tavistock.

Foucault, M. (1970) *The Order of Things: An Archaeology of the Human Sciences*. London: Tavistock.

Foucault, M. (1972) *The Archaeology of Knowledge*. London: Tavistock.

Foucault, M. (1973) *The Birth of the Clinic: An Archaeology of Medical Perception*. London: Tavistock.

Foucault, M. (1979) *Discipline and Punish: The Birth of the Prison*. Harmondsworth: Penguin.

Foucault, M. (1981) *The History of Sexuality: An Introduction*. Harmondsworth: Penguin.

Foucault, M. (1984) *The Use of Pleasure: The History of Sexuality Vol 2*. Harmondsworth: Penguin.

Frobel, F. et.al (1988) *The New International Division of Labour*. Cambridge University Press.

Fryer, P. (1984) *Staying Power*. London: Pluto Press.

Garcia-Castano, F. J. and Moyano, R. A. P. (1993) 'Multicultural Education: Some Reflections on the Spanish Case' in *European Journal of Intercultural Studies*, 4, 2, pp 67-80.

Gellner, E. (1992) *Postmodernism, Reason and Religion*. London: Routledge and Kegan Paul.

Gellner, E. (1985) *Nations and Nationalism*. Oxford; Blackwell.

Giddens, A. (1991) *Modernity and Self-Identity: Self and Society in the Late Modern Age*. Cambridge: Polity Press.

Gieseck, A et al (1994) Economic Implications of Migration into the Federal Republic of Germany 1988-1992' in Spencer, S. (ed) (1994) *Immigration as an Economic Asset: The German Experience*. Stoke-on-Trent: Trentham Books.

Gillwald, K. et al. (1992) Futures. Special Issue: Central and East European Futures. Oxford: Butterworth-Heinemann.

Giroux, H. (1992) 'Postmodernism and the discourse of educational criticism' in Aronowitz, S. and Giroux, H. (1991) *Postmodern Education: Politics, Culture and Social Criticism*. London: University of Minnesota Press.

Gleick, J. (1987). *Chaos: Making a New Science*. London: Abacus.

Goodman, D. (ed) (1991) *Science in Europe 1500-1800. Vol. 2*. Milton Keynes: Open University Press.

Goodman, D. and Russell, C. (eds) (1991) *The Rise of Scientific Europe 1500-1800*. London: Hodder and Stoughton.

Grant, N. (1993) 'The Scots leid an ither wee toungs' [unpublished mss.]

Grant, N. (1994) 'Multicultural Societies in the European Community — the Odd Case of Scotland' in *European Journal of Intercultural Studies*. 5, 1, pp 51-59.

Green, A. (1991). *Education and State Formation. The Rise of Educational Systems in England, France and the USA*. London: Macmillan.

Green, A. (1994) 'Postmodernism and State Education' in *Journal of Education Policy*, 9, 1, pp.67-83.

Hale, J. (1993) *The Civilisation of Europe in the Renaissance*. London: Harper Collins.

Hall, S. et al. (eds.) (1992) *Modernity and its Futures*. Cambridge: Polity Press.

Hargreaves, A. (1994) 'Restructuring: Postmodernity and the Prospects for Educational Change' in *Journal of Education Policy*, 9, 1, pp.47-65.

Harvey, D. (1981) 'The urban process under capitalism: a framework for analysis.' in Dear, M and Scott, M. (ed) (1981) *Urbanisation and Urban Planning in Capitalist Society*. London: Methuen.

Harvey, D. (1989) *The Condition of Postmodernity: An Enquiry into the Origins of Cultural Change*. Oxford: Blackwell.

Harvie, C. (1994) *The Rise of Regional Europe*. London: Routledge and Kegan Paul.

Herrmann, U. (1993) 'Where is the future?' in *Education*, Vol. 48. Institute for Scientific Co-operation, Tubingen

Hewitt, R. (1986) *White Talk, Black Talk: Inter-racial friendship and Communication Amongst Adolescents*. Cambridge: CUP.

Higgins, A. (1994) 'Moscow asserts authority over former empire.' *The Independent*, 13 January 1994, p.13.

Himes, C. (1973) *The Quality of Hurt: The Autobiography of Chester Himes*. London: Michael Joseph.

Hirst, P. (1975) 'The nature and structure of curriculum objectives' in Golby, M. et al. (eds) *Curriculum Design*. London: Croom Helm.

Hodge, R. and Kress, G. (1993) *Language as Ideology*. London: Routledge and Kegan Paul. (Second Edition.)

Hollister, C. (1964) *Medieval Europe*. New York: John Wiley.

Hostermark Tarrou, A-L. (1993) 'The Goals of Enhancing National and International Cultures. Challenges to Teacher Education' in *European Journal of Teacher Education*, 16, 2, pp 95-112.

Illich, I. (1976) *Limits to Medicine: Medical Nemesis: The Expropriation of Health*. Harmondsworth: Penguin.

ILEA. (Inner London Education Authority.) (1983a) *Race, Sex and Class I. Achievement in Schools*. London: ILEA.

ILEA. (Inner London Education Authority.) (1983b) *Race, Sex and Class: 2 Multi-Ethnic Education in Schools*. London: ILEA.

ILEA. (Inner London Education Authority.) (1983c) *Race, Sex and Class 3: A Policy for Equality: Race*. London: ILEA.

ILEA. (Inner London Education Authority.) (1983d) *Race, Sex and Class 4: Anti-Racist Statement and Guidelines*. London: ILEA.

ILEA. (Inner London Education Authority.) (1983e) *Race, Sex and Class 5: Multi-Ethnic Education in Further, Higher and Community Education*. London: ILEA.

ILEA. (Inner London Education Authority.) (1985) *Race, Sex and Class 6: A policy for Equality: Sex*. London: ILEA.

ILEA. (Inner London Education Authority.) (1989) *Prospects for education in Inner london after 1990*. London: ILEA.

Inglis, F. (1973) 'Townscape and popular culture' in Raynor, J and Harden, J. (eds.) (1973) *Cities Communities and the Young*. London: Routledge and Kegan Paul.

James, C. L. R. (1963) *The Black Jacobins*. London: Hutchinson.

Jameson, F. (1991) *Postmodernism or the Cultural Logic of Late Capitalism*. London: Verso.

Jencks, C. et al (1972) *Inequality: A reassessment of the Effect of Family and Schooling in America*. New York: Basic Books.

Jones, C. (1992) 'Cities, diversity and education' in Coulby, D. and Jones, C. (eds) (1992) *The World Yearbook of Education: 1992 Urban Education*. London: Kogan Page.

Jones, K. (1989) *Right Turn: The Conservative Revolution in Education*. London: Hutchinson Radius.

Joseph, G. G. (1992) *The Crest of the Peacock: Non-European Roots of Mathematics*. Harmondsworth: Penguin.

Kamin, L. J. (1974) *The Science and Politics of IQ*. New York: John Wiley.

Karabel, J. and Halsey, A. (eds) (1977) *Power and Ideology in Education*. New York: Oxford University Press.

Kasabova, S. (1991) *Teachers Pack on Somalia*. London: Camden LEA Language Development Service.

Kennedy, P. (1989). *The Rise and Fall of the Great Powers*. London: Fontana Press.

Kepel, G. (1993) *The Revenge of God: the Resurgence of Islam, Christianity and Judaism in the Modern World*. London: Polity Press.

King, A.D. (1990a) *Urbanism, Colonialism and the World Economy: Cultural and Spatial Foundations of the World Urban System*. London: Routledge.

King, A.D.(1990b) *Global Cities: Post-Imperialism and the Internationalisation of London*. London: Routledge.

King, A. D. (1990c) 'Architecture, Capital and the Globalisation of Culture' in Featherstone, M. (ed) (1990) *Global Culture: Nationalism, Globalisation and Modernity. A Theory, Culture and Society Special Issue*. London: Sage.

Kostof, S. (1993) *The City Assembled: The Elements of Urban Form Through History*. London: Thames and Hudson.

Langdon, J. (1995) 'Antwerp's Blok vote.' *The Independent*, 10 January, 1995, p.18.

Lane, J. E. and Ersson, S. O. (1991) *Politics and Society in Western Europe*. (Second Edition) London: Sage.

Lammers, E. (1993) 'Intercultural Education: a Danish Point of View' in *European Journal of Intercultural Studies*, 4, 2, pp 29- 39.

Leavis, F. R. (1962) *The Great Tradition*. Harmondsworth: Penguin.

Leavis, F. R. (1963) *New Bearings in English Poetry*. Harmondsworth: Penguin.

Leavis, F. R. (1964) *D.H. Lawrence/Novelist*. Harmondsworth: Penguin.

Lee, D. (1992) *Competing Discourses: Perspectives and Ideology in Language*. London: Longman.

Lee, D. and Newby, H. (1983) *The Problem of Sociology: An Introduction to the Discipline*. London: Hutchinson.

Liauzu, C. (1994) 'Interculturalism: New Lands to Discover in France' in *European Journal of Intercultural Studies*, 4, 3, pp 25-31.

Lillis, K.M. (1992) 'Urbanisation and Education in Nairobi' in Coulby, D. and Jones, C. (eds) (1992) *The 1992 World Yearbook of Education: Education and Urbanisation*. London: Kogan Page.

Lyotard, J. F. (984) *The Postmodern Condition: A Report on Knowledge*. Manchester: Manchester University Press.

McLean, M. (ed) (1989) *Education in Cities: International Perspectives*. London: British Comparative and International Education Society.

McLean, M. (1990) *Britain and a Single Market Europe: Prospects for a Common School Curriculum*. London: Kogan Page.

McLellan, D. (ed) (1977) *Karl Marx: Selected Writings*. London: Oxford University Press.

McWilliam, E. (1993) "Post' Haste: Plodding Research and Galloping Theory' in *British Journal of Sociology of Education*, 14, 2, pp.199-205.

Mahbub ul-Haq (1994) 'The New Deal'. *New Internationalist*, Number 262, pp 20-23.

Marcou, G. (1993) 'Intercultural Education in Multicultural Greece' in *European Journal of Intercultural Studies*, 4, 3, pp 32-43.

Marr, A. (1993) 'The case for trying to bully the bully' in *The Independent*, 25 March 1993.

Marshall, O. (1991) *Ship of Hope* London: Ethnic Communities Oral History Project et al.

Martenson, J. (1992) *Report to the Director-General on a Mission to Slovenia and Croatia* Paris: UNESCO.

Martiniello, M. and Manco, A. (1993) 'Intercultural Education in French-speaking Belgium: an Overview of Ideology, Legislation and Practice' in *European Journal of Intercultural Studies*, 4, 2, pp 19-27.

Millat, G. (1993) 'Britain and European Integration through British History Schoolbooks Published Between 1961 and 1971' in *European Journal of Teacher Education*, 16, 2, pp.125-136.

Montaigne, M.E. de, (1965) *Essays*. Translated by Florio, J. Three volumes. London: Dent.

Moseley, C and Asher, R. (eds) (1994) *Atlas of the World's Languages*. London: Routledge.

Mortimore, P. et al. (1988) *School Matters: The Junior Years*. Wells: Open Books.

Mortimore, J. and Blackstone, T. (1982) *Disadvantage and Education*. London: Heinemann.

Mumford, L. (1961) *The City in History*. London: Secker and Warburg.

Munck, T. (1990) *Seventeenth Century Europe: State, Conflict and the Social Order in Europe 1598-1700*. Basingstoke: Macmillan.

Murray, J. (ed) (1933) *The Oxford English Dictionary*. Oxford: OUP/Clarendon Press.

Noin, D. and Woods, R. (eds) (1993) *The Changing Population of Europe*. Oxford: Blackwell.

Nundy, J. (1994). 'New ruling on headscarves angers Muslims in France'. *The Independent*, 15 September 1994, p.10.

OECD, Directorate for Social Affairs, Manpower and Education. (1987 to date) *SOPEMI: Continuous reporting system on migration 1986* [to date]. Paris; OECD.

Orr, D. (1992) *Ecological Literacy:Education and the Transition to a Postmodern World*. Albany: State University of New York Press.

Orr, D. (1993) 'Schools for the Twenty-First Century', *Resurgence:* 160, pp 16-19.

Overbye, D. (1991). *Lonely Hearts of the Cosmos: the Quest for the Secret of the Universe*. London: Picador.

Paci, M. (1977) 'Education and the capitalist labor market' in Karabel, J. and Halsey, A. (eds) (1977) *Power and Ideology in Education*. New York: Oxford University Press.

Parker-Jenkins, M. (1994) 'Islam shows its diverse identities', *Times Educational Supplement*, 21 October, 1994, p.13.

Pederson, K. (1993) 'The cultural and linguistic diversity in the Danish German border region.' in *European Journal of Intercultural Studies*, Vol. 3, No. 2/3.

Pederson, R. (1992) *One Europe — 100 Nations*. Clevedon: Multilingual Matters Ltd.

Pesic, V. (1994) 'Bellicose Virtues in Elementary School Readers' in Rosandic, R. and Pesic, V. (eds) (1994) *Warfare, Patriotism, Patriarchy: The Analysis of Elementary School Textbooks*. Belgrade: Centre for Anti-War Action MOST.

Pick, D. (1993) *War Machine: the Rationalisation of Slaughter in the Modern Age*. New Haven: Yale University Press

Pilger, J. (1994) East Timor: The Silence and The Betrayal. *New Internationalist*, Number 253. March 1994.

Popper, K. R. (1966a) *The Open Society and Its Enemies. Vol. 1 The Spell of Plato*. London: Routledge and Kegan Paul.

Popper, K. R. (1966b) *The Open Society and Its Enemies. Vol. 2 The High Tide of Prophecy: Hegel, Marx and the Aftermath*. London: Routledge.

Popper, K. R. (1972) *Conjunctures and Refutations: The Growth of Scientific Knowledge*. London: Routledge and Kegan Paul.

Pound, E. (1938) *Guide to Kulchur*. London: Peter Owen.

Pound, E. (1954) *Literary Essays of Ezra Pound*. London: Faber.

Pyke, N. (1994) 'Discontentment in Search of a Voice', *Times Educational Supplement*, 21 October, 1994, p.12.

Rabinow, P. (1989) *French Modern: Norms and Forms of the Social Environment.* Harvard: MIT Press.

Radcliffe, P. (1992) "Britain' and 'Europe': an exploration of conceptual confusions.' in *European Journal of Intercultural Studies*, 3, 1,pp.28-34.

Rafferty, F. (1994) 'Historians clash over Nationalism', *Times Educational Supplement*, 4 November, 1994, p.18.

Rattansi, A. (1994)"Western' racisms, ethnicities and Identities in a 'postmodern' frame.' in Rattansi, A. and Westwood, S. (1994) (Eds.) *Racism, Modernity and Identity on the Western Front.* Cambridge: Polity Press.

Rattansi, A. and Westwood, S. (1994) (Eds.) *Racism, Modernity and Identity on the Western Front.* Cambridge: Polity Press.

Reich, H.H. (1994) 'Intercultural Education in Germany' in *European Journal of Intercultural Studies* 4, 3, pp 14-24.

Rhodes, R. (1988) *The Making of the Atomic Bomb.* Harmondsworth: Penguin.

Roberts, J.M. (1980) *The Pelican History of the World.* Harmondsworth: Penguin.

Robinson, C. (1983) *Black Marxism: the Making of the Black Radical Tradition.* London: Zed Press.

Rodney, W. (1972) *How Europe Underdeveloped Africa.* London: Bogle L'Ouverture.

Rogers, R. (1993) 'Common Core History for Young Europeans' in *European Journal of Teacher Education*, 16, 2, pp.113-124.

Rosandic, R. and Pesic, V. (eds) (1994) *Warfare, Patriotism, Patriarchy: The Analysis of Elementary School Textbooks.* Belgrade: Centre for Anti-War Action/MOST.

Rushdie, S. (1988) *The Satanic Verses.* London: Viking.

Russell, J. (c.1838) *A Complete Atlas of the World.* London: Fisher, Son and Co.

Rutter, M. et al (1979) *Fifteen Thousand Hours.* London: Open Books.

Rutter, J. (1991) *Refugees: We Left Because We Had To.* London: The Refugee Council.

Rutter, J. (1994) *Refugee Children in the Classroom.* Stoke-on- Trent: Trentham Books.

Rutter, J. and Fischer, A. (1992) *Refugees from Bosnia, Serbia and Croatia.* London: The Refugee Council.

Said, E. (1993) *Culture and Imperialism.* London : Chatto and Windus.

Saunders, P. (1981) *Social Theory and the Urban Question*. London: Hutchinson.

Schneider, H-G. (1989) 'Nationalism in eighteenth-century German chemistry' in Goodman, D. and Russell, C. (eds) (1991) *The Rise of Scientific Europe 1500-1800*. London: Hodder and Stoughton.

Sharma, S. (1989) *Citizens: a Chronicle of the French Revolution*. Harmondsworth: Penguin.

Sharma, S. (1991) *The Embarrassment of Riches*. London: Fontana Press.

Shennan, M. (1991) *Teaching About Europe*. London: Cassell.

Shyllon, F. (1977) *Black People in Britain, 1555-1833*. Oxford: OUP.

Simpson, J. and Weiner, E. [Eds.] (1989 onward) *Oxford English Dictionary*. [Second Edition] Oxford: OUP/Clarendon Press.

Sivanandan, A. (1988) 'The new racism' *New Statesman and Society*, 4 November 1988.

Singleton, F. (1985) *A Short History of the Yugoslav Peoples*. Cambridge: CUP.

Skutnabb-Kangas, T. and Cummins, J. (1988) *Minority Education: from Shame to Struggle*. Clevedon: Multilingual Matters.

Skutnabb-Kangas, T. (1990) *Language, Literacy and Minorities*. London: Minority Rights Group.

Smith, A. D. (1990) 'Towards a Global Culture?' in Featherstone, M. (ed) (1990) *Global Culture: Nationalism, Globalisation and Modernity. A Theory, Culture and Society Special Issue*. London: Sage.

Somali Relief Association] (SOMRA) (1991) *The Somalis: an Invisible Community in Crisis*. London: SOMRA

Sorokin, P. and Zimmerman, C. (1929) *Principles of Rural-Urban Sociology*. New York: Hinny-Holt.

Spencer, S. (ed) (1994) *Immigration as an Economic Asset: The German Experience*. London: Trentham Books.

Spender, D. (1980) *Man Made Language*. London: Routledge and Kegan Paul.

Stojanovic, D. (1994) 'History Text Books Mirror their Time' in Rosandic, R. and Pesic, V. (eds) (1994) *Warfare, Patriotism, Patriarchy: The Analysis of Elementary School Textbooks*. Belgrade: Centre for Anti-War Action/MOST.

Street-Porter, R. (1977) *Race, Children and Cities*. Milton Keynes: Open University Press.

Swift, R. (1994) Squeezing the South. *New Internationalist*, Number 257, July 1994.

Szabio, L.T. (1993) 'Values and Value Conflicts in Hungarian Education: The Case of the National Core Curriculum — an Unfinished Story' in *European Journal of Intercultural Studies*, 4, 1, 57-64.

Szaday, C. (1994) 'Schooling in Multicultural Switzerland' in *European Journal of Intercultural Studies*, 5, 1, pp 38-50.

Thomas, W.B. and Moran, K.J. 'Urban decline and Educational Opportunities in Secondary Schools of Pittsburgh. Pennsylvania, 1950-79' in Coulby, D. and Jones, C. (eds) (1992) *The World Yearbook of Education 1992: Education and Urbanisation*. London: Kogan Page.

Thurrow, L. (1972) 'Education and economic equality.' in Karabel, J. and Halsey, A. (eds) (1977) *Power and Ideology in Education*. New York: Oxford University Press.

The Times Atlas of the World: Family Edition. (1991) London: Times Books.

Tierney, J. (ed) (1982) *Race, Migration and Schooling*. London: Holt Reinhart Winston.

Tierney, J. (1982) 'Race, colonisation and migration' in Tierney, J. (1982) (ed) *Race, Migration and Schooling*. London:Holt, Reinhart and Winston.

Trindade, M.B.R. and Medes, M.L.S. (1993) 'Portugal: a Profile of Intercultural Education' in *European Journal of Intercultural Studies*, 4, 2, pp 59-65.

United Nations [UN] (1951) *Convention Relating to the Status of Refugees*. New York: UN.

United Nations (UN) (1967) *Protocol Relating to the Status of Refugees*. New York: UN.

Usher, R. and Edwards, R. (1994) *Postmodernism and Education*. London: Routledge.

Van Boven, T. (1993) 'The European Context for Intercultural Education'. *European Journal of Intercultural Studies*, 4, 1, 7- 14.

Warner, R. [Ed.] (1991) *Codad Ka Yimi Soomaaliya/Voices from Somalia*. London: Minority Rights Group.

Whitty, G. and Young, M. (eds) (1976) *Explorations in the Politics of School Knowledge*. Driffield: Nafferton.

Williams, E. (1984) 'Painting by numbers?' *Times Higher Educational Supplement*, 28 October, 1994, pp.15-16.

Williams, R. (1981) *Culture*. London: Fontana.

Witteck, F. et al (1993) 'Cultural and Linguistic Diversity in the Education Systems of the European Community' in *European Journal of Intercultural Studies*, 4, 2, pp 7-17.

Young, M.F.D. (ed) (1971) *Knowledge and Control*. London: Collier- Macmillan.

Zukin, S. (1988) *Loft Living: Culture and Capital in Urban Change*. London: Radius.

Zukin, S. (1991) *Landscapes of Power: From Detroit to Disney World*. Berkeley: University of California Press.

INDEX

Aims of education 80
Architecture 1, 137
Assimilation 94, 112-113, 122

'Back to Basics' 144-145
Bernal, M. 103-104

Capitalism 5
CDPs 146
Chaos theory 8
Christianity 8-9, 19-21, 41, 48-49, 70, 80, 130
Cities 59-69, 107, 139
    Rural-urban dichotomy 65-67, 119
    Semiology of cities 64-66
    Urban education 63, 121, 134, 141-142
Community education 71-72
Cornish 92
Cultural relativism 102-105, 130-131
Cultural studies 1
Curriculum 16, 23-26, 31-31, 37-38, 42, 72-76, 107, 138-139
    Cannons 29-30
    European 42, 99, 127-133, 135, 138-139

Geography 57
History 20-22, 74-76, 132-133, 136-137
Literature 29
Mathematics 104-105, 137
Science 27-28, 57, 109, 111
see also Language

Differentiation 83-86, 89
Discrimination 95

Education and economy 15, 80
Education Reform Act, 1988 38, 142
EPAs 146
Ethnocentricism 95, 102, 104, 107
Europe
    Canons 29-30, 69, 96, 99
    Civic culture 59-77
    Concepts of Europe 9, 41-50, 86, 129
    Concepts of European identity 9, 31, 41-43, 50-57
    Eurocentricism 34-35, 42, 56, 102-104
    History 7-9, 54, 97, 132
    Turkey 48-49, 55, 57

165

Feminism 33-34

Gender 37, 99-100
    Curriculum issues 17, 33
Gypsies 12, 20-21, 120, 134

HIV/AIDS 8
Holocaust 9, 21, 137
Human rights 79-81

Identity 82-83, 88
Intelligence, concepts of 87-88
Intercultural education 37-38, 57, 83,
    86, 135-136
    Taxonomies 111-114, 122
Information technology 3, 90
Islam 7-9, 19, 48-49, 70-71, 130, 134

Language 17-18, 53-54, 73, 76,
    134-136
    Bilingualism/Multilingualism
        18, 76, 89, 93-94, 123, 131
    Language loss 17-18, 90-92
    Literacy 17
    Sign language 92
London 92, 121-123, 132, 134-137

'Others', The 2, 33

Market, the educational 144
Manx 92
Marxism 5, 8, 25
Maastricht Treaty 118, 127, 129
Medicine 8, 105
Migratory patterns 118-119, 133-134
Minorities, definitions of 81-83, 113,
    117
Modernist knowledge systems
    100-102

Museums and galleries 35-36
Music 105

Nation state 52-53

Pyrrhonism 7

Racism 12, 21, 56
Refugees 112, 116-125
Religion 7-8, 19-21, 70-71, 83, 99, 134,
    143
    see also Christianity, Islam

School effectiveness 146
Stereotypes 15

Textbooks 8
Tourism 5
Traditionalist knowledge systems
    99-100

Underachievement 13-14
UN Convention on the Rights of the
    Child 81
USSR 91-92, 98, 120, 142, 147

War 8
    Franco-Prussian 8
    Gulf 108
    Spanish Civil 107, 120
    World War I 8, 52, 54, 74, 107
    World War II 8, 52, 120
Welsh 92, 97, 122, 132-133

Xenophobia 107, 122, 147